for Barry — you ran out of time here, but not out of influence.

UNDO

How to undo the past and plan your future

by Matthew Powell

ISBN- 9780988321670

Check out other titles at http://Pramek.com

License Notes

This book is licensed for your personal enjoyment only. This book may not be re-sold. If you would like to share this book with another person, please purchase an additional copy or ask for permission from the author. If you're reading this book and did not purchase it, or it was not purchased for your use only, then please return to Pramek.com and purchase your own copy.

Table of Contents

The first time I rented out a beach house it had been 8 years since I had taken a vacation. I piled my dogs into my old 4Runner, drove down, and did absolutely nothing but write for a while. After years of working in a good career while running successful online businesses and teaching around the world for nearly two decades...I was exhausted. So, I spent my mornings running, my days on the beach, and my nights covered in drunk on the couch, covered in aloe, watching some show about people repossessing cars. The next year I once again piled the dogs in the Land Cruiser, along with my dogs, Phoenix and Patton (RIP to both), and drove down to the beach house again.

As they sat on the beach, soaking in the sun, I started this book (along with three others) on a wobbly table poised atop the deck overlooking the ocean. My previous year's nights drunk on margaritas and aloe covered couch sits were replaced with wine and nice dinners though I did manage to take in some trash TV shows while we were there. I had planned out the year before to have a better, bigger vehicle, to open myself up to a relationship, spend a little less time working and a little more time enjoying life. And, well, there I was doing it but my mind never stops for long and I decided I would try to teach other people how to enjoy their lives.

An idea I had been toying with for a while, about changing the concept of what martial art 'is', began to take hold in typed word and scrawled notes. I started a planning book, a guide to new college graduates book, a book about management (with a huge twist) and of course, a martial art book. A year later, the guide to new graduates 90% completed, the management book 90% completed, and the martial art book now three books (each about 45 pages), I decided the planning book would be the first to release. Being able to plan was the cornerstone for post-graduation and for management, and for anyone who studies or teaches martial arts. At 45% complete I bared down and with a workbook not even in my mind, I switched gears. What's the point of the other books if you can't plan what to do with the information you learn?

As I write this I am known for my martial arts and what I have done with the system I have created. It wasn't easy but I built an international organization, developed a new way of teaching that many schools have adopted, and made a lot of friends along the way. I trained with some of the great teachers, am still in awe of some of the things I've seen and done. Most of all I'm thankful to God each day that I have accomplished some pretty neat stuff so far. In my business life I have been just as successful, rising from the literal bottom to the top of what I want to do...I planned the rise years before. I decided what I would do and have made every step of the way happen. From working with self-made millionaires to billion-dollar corporation war rooms, I've learned a lot. I've also failed a lot, and fast, been unsuccessful more times than successful, and spent many nights wondering who is staring back at me in the mirror and why he keeps going when I would rather quit.

I decided to design this book like I would teach the methods in it to a class - the editors hate this kind of work, but I love it. After teaching thousands on multiple continents and people still asking me to teach, I think I'm pretty good at it. So, I wrote it for you. I am hoping that I will be recognized for more than what I have done in martial art, where I have taught people to survive, and will be known for what I do beyond...teaching people to live to their fullest.

If you enjoy it, spread the word, and most of all...spread encouragement.

And btw...the workbook, it's in the back of the book.

- M

Wrong goals, right process...

The first time I gave someone this book to review they laughed and said, 'Is all of this really necessary? Is it really that hard to plan out your goals?'

This is a successful guy saying this. It's a guy who makes a lot (lot!) of money as an entrepreneur, so when someone like that questions your work about being successful, well, you better have a good answer. So, I asked him in reply, 'How many New Year's goals did you set this year?'

'Ten or fifteen, I think' he said, still looking at the book in front of him.

I smiled as I asked my next questions, '10 or 15 you think? How many did you achieve?'

He looked down at the book, then as his feet, then said with a chuckle, 'Two or three, maybe?'

'Two or three maybe? And the year before?' I asked.

'The same, maybe less. Maybe...ok Matt, ok, ok, I need your book.'

I really dislike planning books but what I dislike even more is not living the best life I can. So, over the years I created a planning system for myself. It took a lot of what I knew about what makes billion dollar businesses run, self-made entrepreneurs successful, and my thousands of students over the year. This isn't a 'write a few goals, say a mantra about how great you are, go out there and achieve' book.

This is an experience you're about to do.

How do I know?

Because it changed me when I did it.

You know your creation is good when it changes you! I did the typical goal planning before. I made a list, wrote some goals, decided what I would do to achieve the goals. I even bought some books on planning and personal growth. Like anyone else I have spent my time in the car listening to books on tape, getting pumped up to a great teacher. I went to some seminars. I even talked to a well-known 'life coach' who told me to make sure I made my goals SMART, which is the acronym for specific, measurable, and so on. This all made sense and it seemed, according to everyone, that this was the way to achieve my goals. I was going to be a success, donncha ya know! Everyone told me I would attain success! Then I wondered a basic question:

What if I've chosen the wrong goals?

Uh-oh.

The right process for the wrong goals would only lead me in the wrong direction.

I thought, 'You mean I just spent a year making sure I was measurable and assignable to something I never should have chosen in the first place?' I have seen this happen in corporate boardrooms where a company will use every business process known to man to make the perfect case for the wrong product. This happens in people's lives as well when they are set on courses based on yesterday's mindset trying to achieve today's goals. No one ever tells you that you might choose the wrong goals because no one wants to tell you that you are wrong. You won't come back if you get told you're wrong, or you failed, right? At least that's what my editor told me when I sent the rough-draft over and he replied back, 'I don't know if you want to tell people they fail - maybe a different word?' Everyone is so caught up in people coming back that they don't worry about where they are sending people to. I told the editor no thanks (so forgive any errors), I'd do this on my own, self-publish, and not be second guessed on words. So we will do this on our own, you and I, and we'll come out better on the other end.

They say the best way out of a tough situation is through it. Your life, up until this point, may have been one big tough situation. But, as you'll see in this book, this isn't chance and it isn't luck. It's you - you're the problem and you're the solution. You made it all happen and you can make something else happen. The words 'it' and 'something' could mean massive success or gigantic failure, but regardless, you'll make it happen. Most people would stop right there, tell you to go succeed, and then hope you come back. Me, I'm a little different. After spending almost two decades teaching people how to do everything from move better to kill people (neither of which you can teach remotely on occasionally), I'm going to be in this with you. While I'm not there in the room with you, I can be there in how I write this book, it's structure, how I guide you through it, and how I make myself available to help you with it.

There will be points in this book and workbook where you will think about stopping. I almost stopped once, beyond planning...I decided to stop everything. I was on the top of my game in martial art, business, my job, relationships, even my dogs were behaving awesome...and I lost the fire. I wanted to quit because I felt no matter how much I succeeded it wouldn't be enough. Not monetarily - I have more than enough money and ways to make more. Not fame - I am known by the people I want to be known by. It was about my legacy and what I was leaving behind. At every turn someone would try to steal it, someone would compare me to someone else and belittle my work, or some anonymous troll would bash me on the internet. It seemed everything conspired against my confidence and you'll be no different. I had to make some radical changes to my thought process which you will read about in another book.

The process we are about to do, this undertaking of change, is going to conspire against your confidence. We are going to work hard to undo the past. What do I mean by 'undo'? It's more than just a book title. The process will make you admit things you don't want to admit and relive things you would prefer not to relive. It will ask you to choose what's important and what's not. It's going to make you ask people for help and get rejected. Most powerfully, it will encourage you to choose who should be part of your life and who shouldn't. Only by doing this can you undo the past and its hold on you. Undo isn't the same as redo or unmake. We can't go back in time and we can't make what happened not happen. But the past has a way of making us into who we are. As you'll see with the concept of themes, the past has a way of making you do things you don't even know you are doing. So, I asked myself, 'what if I could undo this? What if I could start fresh when I chase my new goals?' It's like taking off glasses that have an old prescription or taking off old shoes that don't fit anymore. Life is similar with most people squinting and limping through it and on occasion they see clearly or walk proudly. You don't know how bad things were until you have a contrast to them. We have to develop that contrast so we remember how things were. We have to remember that contrast so we can appreciate the changes we make. When you do this, when you develop the contrast and remember it, you can begin to undo the past and its hold on you.

So it doesn't matter the year you had or what's wrong with your life, we will turn that into the past and it is going to take fortitude. So I'll tell you - you are tough, you are smart, you are capable - but you also fail, you make mistakes, and you have habits that are messing up your life. But that's you, who you are today, and the great thing about life...you can change at any time.

Now, let's get to changing...

Phase 1: Reflection

I've traveled cross-country many times in my life, from NYC to Arco Idaho, home of the world's first nuclear power plant. With all of this travel I can tell you one thing: directions change with each person you ask. Some say 'left', others say 'right', some say 'forward' while others say 'straight'. I grew up in the south where directions were usually personal and very confusing, 'Go to the sign, past the fork in the road, take a right at that fork, then after you pass that sign, go past Mr. Strickland's house. If he's outside wave at him or he'll thrown things at your car. Once you go past Mr. Strickland's, you'll go past an old cemetery. My grandmother is buried in that cemetery and lemme tell you about her...' Hard to follow is the best way to explain most of the directions we get in life. In the majority of cases we'd be better off with maps, GPS, and an address.

The older we get the more we realize those kinds of directions hold a lot of value because they make you a better traveler. You learn the back roads, history, and gain knowledge of why you take particular routes and not others. Then, the next time you go down that road you know all of this information, it makes the trip easier, and if someone is with you, a more interesting traveling companion. But, the roads change, Mr. Strickland's house disappears over the years, and before long the cemetery headstones will weather with rain and time. If years pass between visits, then familiar places can seem to be foreign countries with the changes that happen.

Personal planning is very similar. If you don't know where you came from it's hard to develop a plan for where you will go. Once on the road it becomes easy to forget where you are going as you stop off at all the shops and scenic views along the way. You also must ask questions about why are you are on the trip, what kind of car you have, and who are you traveling with. As we look at life and try to determine how we will achieve success and leave a legacy we tell ourselves, 'if only life had an instructional manual! If only I had life's map!'

While life doesn't come with an instructional manual, it offers teachers to show you along the way. As for a map we have our experience and planning. Experience is the map we've used and planning is how we make sense of our experience. Our old map is usually missing pieces, names may be worn off, areas scribbled out or you've written a note such as 'don't go back there.' Once we get on the road everything you've known can become worthless and perhaps even harmful if the world has changed. Many stick with that map and become lost in a life based on the past. The successful folks recognize the we can create a new map, choose a new destination, new car, new traveling companions!

But, before we go Thelma and Louise on life and build the new map we first need to grab the old map.... there might be information we can keep to make the journey easier. That knowledge about why the road is the way it is and how it used to be. We have to look back at the valuable information we found out going the wrong way or taking the right path. Grabbing that old map means looking at the past and learning from it through a process of reflection.

The end point
Reflection is a two-step process. Discovering our successes and failures first, then becoming uncomfortable with them second. Pain is a powerful teacher which means experiencing discomfort is important so we find out what comfort is.

So, what about those successes and failures?

As we get started let's talk terminology. We have to make sure both have the same definition of the words being used or we won't get very far! The first thing I need you to realize, in planning, a success or a failure is a moment in time - an event, and that's it. The people there, your feelings, emotions, even the music playing happened during that event. The event is not the same as the memory of the event. As time goes on your memory of the event will change which is why we have to look at the event differently. It's doubtful you remember your successes or failures as a 5-year-old which speaks to their fleeting nature. You can't go back and repeat a success, or get a failure do-over...you can only remember what it was like and then try to replicate it. You'll never have that same success again. We have to focus on all the things making up the event that the success happened in.

In this book we will refer to them as events (you'll see why, I promise) and I want to make sure you understand it's only a moment in time. See success and failure as a single instance and that's it. You're not a failure or a success...you are a person who is failing or succeeding. Success doesn't define anyone any more than failure unless they let it define them. I had a mentor, a self-made millionaire, who had a series of successes, but he had one major failure: he did hard drugs at a party once. After that he worried more about partying, which he was successful at, but he was simultaneously a failure at his business as a he made a string of failed decisions. He could change it at any time by taking one failure event, one point in time, and making it a success. But, he didn't...and he lost it all.

Now that we have defined failure and success let's talk about what we are about to do. To get the information you need to change your life you must get uncomfortable and honest. We have all had the occasion when we regret being candid, or someone being honest with us has created an awkward situation. In planning we want to be uncomfortable, candid, and awkward with ourselves. So, don't worry about breaking out the wine or a beer if that helps you loosen up a little. At higher levels of planning you can bring other people into your planning sessions and ask them to double check your work, but for now, it'll be just you.

When you feel like 'it sucks to admit this' you're on the right path. Just remember - an endpoint is not a path. When viewed on a map, Los Angeles is 2180 miles from Atlanta. Los Angeles is the endpoint but the trip I take by plane will be a different path than a train or car. Worry about the path, not the end point because the path is where you get lost. You will one day pass on to the other side...how you get to that endpoint is your path. Some people take exciting paths and some take safe paths, but regardless, one day they all die. It's the stories they tell, their experiences, and their legacy that matters.

What does all this mean?

Success and failure don't care about you - they occur once and then you have to make them occur again. They are events and at any time you can decide to have a different event if you want to. It's all in how you see it. You get to choose who you will become and how you get there, and that takes planning. You can choose your path, and by combining the knowledge that you can choose with the ability to change events from failure to success...you are powerful.

So open your workbook to page 3 and let's get started.

Getting started

If you used this method previously then pull the old workbook out and begin looking through it. Familiarize yourself with your goals from last time, listing what was a failure and a success. Mentally put yourself back into your mind state from your last session and remember the process that went into choosing your goals. Using this information prepare for your free writing session. If you have never used our process before, don't worry, you'll pick it right up.

First a thought exercise to fire up your neurons and get you thinking. What do you feel you failed at or succeeded at in the previous year? What did you accomplish at work or with

14

a hobby? What project did you not win at work? What event gave a sense of pride or regret? Think in terms of your relationships, friends, sports team, and trips you've taken. Close your eyes, think back on the past few months to a year and focus on pride and regret, success and failure, the good times and the bad.

Ready to list your successes and failures?

On pages 3 and 4 you will see open pages for your to free write your successes and failures on.

Free writing is when you write without worrying about structure, grammar, spelling, etc. There are no rules here, no one else will read it and use a red-pen like a teacher when you were younger. It's you, your mind, the pen, and the paper. Free writing is spontaneous. In free writing if a topic you are concentrating on (in this case a success or failure event) pops into your mind, you write it down. Don't block thoughts, just scribble them down. In blocking the thought, you are blocking the exercise. Just write it and move on. Scribble down every success and failure that comes into your head. Don't put a lot of thought into it, just write what you thought about then move on.

If you have never done free writing here are some tips to make it easier:

   - Start with a simple exercise on free writing chores. Take a blank piece of paper and without thinking about it write down everything you need to do today chore wise. Go to the store, clean up the house, send an email...if you have to do it, write it. For 3 minutes try this out and what you will find is you will start remembering things. You will have that 'oh yea' moment. After 3 minutes look at your list. You just did a free writing sessions.

   - After this clear your mind and then visualize the major successes this past year. As you visualize a success, write it down on the corresponding page.

-Start in spurts. Try free writing for 2 minutes on major successes then stop. Take a minute, walk around the room, then come back to the paper. If you have any thoughts that came into your mind while you were walking around quickly scribble them down.

-Now you need to clear your mind. Close your eyes then repeat to yourself out loud, 'I am writing my successes [or failures]. I have nothing in my mind but my successes. I am writing my successes.'

-Begin writing again for 3 minutes. After you have finished, get up, walk around, scribble down your walk around thoughts, then repeat the mantra again.

-When you're done with the mantra write for 4 minutes.

-The point is to exhaust your mind in spurts. You will find as you do the exercise that with each writing section more successes are found, and you weren't even really trying. In free writing it just happens.

-When you come to a point you can no longer find a success to scribble down, stop and walk around before you decide to tackle another topic such as failures.

I recommend starting with your successes. Free write through your successes on page 3. Once you have completed this move on to your failures on Page 4. Take as many pieces of paper needed if the workbook isn't enough. Too much information is never a bad thing if you have a means of deciphering what's important, and luckily, we have that process. Take as many free writing sessions that you feel are warranted until you've exhausted your mind and memory onto the pages. You might find it therapeutic to spend time without structure and grammar, and if so, you will love this book. Whether it takes one page or five, focus on getting all of the information onto the paper.

When you've completed the free writing for success and failure take a moment and look back over your lists. If you need to organize them, write a little more about certain events, feel free because that's what free writing is for. It's your time without pressure, just you and the paper. Line through the successes, doodle, change a word...it's your writing!

Once you're done I want you to recognize something. What you've just done is very powerful. Most people have little idea who they are or what they can achieve. When you look at the paper, realize something about what you've written:

This is who you were in the past year. For good or bad, this is you.

Questions to Ponder

Take time to fill out the Questions to Ponder on page 5. No, I'm not telling you what to do, but this may help you get an idea of anything you might have overlooked in your free writing. It will also give you a chance to refine your list a little bit. You may find in answering these questions you gain clarity about some of your successes and failures. You may have listed something as a goal but failed, or you could have turned a failure into a success. In this you find you not only failed at accomplishing something, but you might also fail at achieving goals in general, and conversely successes as well.

This overarching success or failure is the parent of your individual events when it comes to goals.

Why is this? There are many factors that come into play in the creation of these events. The timing might not have been right or perhaps something else was more important. In the end these are reasons (something being more important) and excuses (not enough time). When the event is over there is a reality we must realize: at any time we could have done something different. Part of having free-will is embracing the concept that everything is our own making, our decision. Few things in life are outside of our control and when they are out of our control our reaction to those things is within our control.

Most often we fail to make a decision to decide. Ask yourself when, during the day, at a time you face a decision did you take time to decide on what you would do. Did you look at the future and how it would affect the future? Look at your past and think about how the past may affect the decision you might make? All that free will we have to decide what we want and we still rarely make decisions.

We go with the moment, go with the flow, but the flow rarely takes into account how the decision will affect us long term. Part of taking control of one's life is taking control of your brain and making it recognize when you can make a decision. Once you recognize this...you can take all of the information you have in hand and decide the best course. I have a book about this coming in the future so I won't dig deep into the concept, but rest assured, if you decide to make a decision, even on the smallest things, you are taking power over your life.

So, as you fill out the Questions to Ponder, think about how you could have made better decisions that may have made a success more impactful, or turned a failure in a success (you'll hear this again!). After you've reflected on your free written lists with these Questions, turn to page 6.

It's time to transfer your free writing to a more organized list.

Organized Success List

Now we will begin to make some sense of our free writing. Look back at your free writing and let's perform some thought exercises regarding our successes and failures so we gain insight into the events.

Thought Exercise 1: Separation

When you think of a success or failure don't think of it as paragraphs, such as, 'I won the Acme project and then I got promoted but then I failed to secure the XYZ company contract.' Think in terms of events: 'won the Acme project', 'got promoted', 'failed to secure the XZ company contract'. Do you see it now...? You could have lost the Acme project but still gotten promoted and the secured the XYZ contract. As humans we look for patterns so we fail to see our successes and failures as individual events. When you see them individually you realize that you had power over each one of them.

Thought Exercises 2: Refining

Look at each event and ask yourself a few questions. Why was it a success or failure? Are you leaving out details? Could you define it better? Could you reduce it to more or less words that are more direct? For example, 'moved to a bigger house' may be rewritten to the refined list as 'moved from $150K house to $300K house.' You might have bought a new car so ask yourself why you bought the new vehicle. 'Bought a new car' may be refined as 'bought a more fuel-efficient vehicle' or 'bought a vehicle to make family more comfortable.'

It's not enough to list a success or a failure. What made it a success or failure is what it accomplished. You may find insight. A failure such as 'lost biggest sale of the year' may be refined to 'lost biggest sale to XYZ company.' By refining the failure, you see it was to one company and does not reflect all of the other successes you had because you may have landed the second biggest sale of the year (which I hope is listed as a success!). When you refine the list you find insight into your successes and failures. Remember - these are events, one time in your life. Rarely will you remember a success or failure 15 years from now. So take time to refine the success or failure to reflect very direct information.

Having looked at your free written lists let's get ready to transfer them to Organized Success List on page 6 and Organized Failure List on Page 7. When you transfer it over to your workbook don't 'free write it' but make it grammatically correct and neatly written! Ready to transfer?

First, when you list successes or failure that are groupings of events together, separate them up and if need be list the details that made them what they were.

Second, use the process of Refining whenever you can to make your successes and failure clear and concise. Get to the reason behind the reason whenever your transfer the information. Dig deep!

Successes

Below is example of successes I've seen listed over time. As you can see from this list there are many kinds of events in your life to consider a success.

Success

Moved to bigger house
Tried new business ventures
Won sales team of the year
Bought new car
Learned how to use IPad
Traing for half marathon
Got $10,000 more in savings
Won Acme Co project
Started new blog
Gained 300 new instagram followers
Made successful network for blog
Ran two 5 K's
Project featured in industry magazine
Published my first article in magazine
Managed three successful team projects
Developed good attorney relationship
All three kids got straight A's

Failures

This listing is similar to the successes section. As you transfer the list there are some things you should not list repeatedly, like every time you have missed a weekly report at work. Just list it as 'missed weekly targets at work' and move on. And, as one last note in your transfer, even if it was out of your control, list it.

Failures

Didn't learn new language
Didn't run marathon
Lost $5,000 in new investment
Didn't get to goal weight
Didn't have $20,00 in savings
Didn't learn to use photoshop
Felt sluggish from hangovers
Missed multiple project dates
Lost promotion to Janet
Lost $5,000 in initial product release
Didn't go to church twice monthly
Couldn't afford investing (Tom's co)
Cholesterol too high
Didn't clean out garage
Didn't advance in merger
Didn't take international trip
Didn't quit smoking completely

Groups

As a thought exercise determine what you had direct control over, i.e., groups. This is where you need to do some refining to make sure you are honest with yourself.

Think for a moment about any success or failure where you were part of a group. If your department or team won a prize don't list that. List your role within it because the group success is not truly a personal success. You may think, 'But Matt, that was a success, what's the difference!' While it might have been a success, it was only a measure of your ability to be involved in a team success…not do the project yourself. You should only list individual successes or failures even if they happened in an organized group. The goal of this exercise is to make a distinction between personal and team successes and failures. Many times people confuse their personal ability for the ability of a team and fail to grasp their personal strengths and weaknesses. To be successful, you must measure yourself only, alone or in a team. So take a moment, go back and refine any group success you were part of to make sure it reflects only your role.

This may not seem important but you just took a big step. You differentiated between yourself and others, seeing your success as individual. I have seen many businesses and relationships suffer because people can't do this. People see the organization, or the marriage as the problem and forget they are part of the organization's success or failure…and soon they give up hope. Conversely, you may have been part of a group that failed but you succeeded in your role within in the group. This is why we look beyond patterns to individual events. So, congrats, you've taken a big step.

Done?

Once you've transferred your successes and failures take a moment to think about them once more.

Did you cover everything? Did you list it all out?

Good…now it's time to make sense of these lists.

Phase 2: Themes

When I started the concept of Pastless in Pramek, the theme was to help people become successful and happy in life. The methods, such as planning and systems you can follow, my stories, the blog, videos...they all create Pastless. Taken separately they may be effective in different ways but something would be missing. When you tie them together, the exercises, chapters, the workbook, down to the words chosen...they fit within the theme of an overall system of self-growth.

I was once asked to simplify the concept of a theme. Well, I'm a big fan of coffee. Any kind of coffee put in front of me I'll try it and drink it gladly. In my mind, if a coffee is not very good, it only needs a little sugar or cream to reach its full potential. So, while I may have Turkish, Starbucks, or Eight O'clock, I always like it sweet. Sweet is the theme. When you think of themes remember it's the underlying concept behind what you are doing.

Life is very similar. The underlying reasons for your successes and failures are the themes of your actions. Success and failure are individual events by nature but tied together by you and your actions. Concepts such as your habits, your experiences, and your belief in yourself become determining factors for what you achieve in this life. As you pull back from the day to day grind you have to look at life event to event. These events seem separate from each other but you will find that there are themes that exist tying together the events in your life. If you are always late, it's not the events of being late that are the theme but most likely your lack of time management. The action, being late, should not be confused with being late all the time. Lateness must be seen at its root theme, such as lack of time management. Such overarching themes are the reasons we succeed or fail, not the individual success or failure event itself. In life we think, 'right place, right time' or 'wrong time, wrong person.' This leaves much of our lives up to chance, but chance is something we have no control over. If we want true control we have to find out the driving themes behind the individual events, such as why we end up in the right place at the right time.

Discovering your themes

Many people would say 'look at who, what, when, where, why', or the 5W's, and this may seem self-evident in discovering a theme. Unfortunately, the who, what, when, where, and why are singular in their nature. A theme leads us to arrive at the right or wrong 'W' in time. A theme is separate from the 'who' or 'what'. 'Who' themes are not *a* person, but knowing the *right* people. 'When' themes are not the times you invest, but when and how you came to know the right time to invest.

Let's say you've had difficult legal battles this year you were successful in winning. There may be a tendency to list the relationship with your attorney, for example Julie, as a theme. She was there at every success right? But, what would happen if Julie vanished from the face of the earth tomorrow? What is it about Julie that makes her so important? What role does she play and what does she stand for? What about Julie's background or personality makes her successful as your attorney? Could you find more people like Julie if she did actually vanish tomorrow?

Finding another Julie is a what the relationship with Julie represents and not Julie herself. In this case, 'good relationships with attorneys' would be a possible theme. While you might not find another Julie, you can find an attorney who represents what Julie means to your life. Another example may be stocks you picked to invest in...the theme is not the stocks. The theme is the knowledge to pick the stocks. As you dig deeper you might find recognition of how you came to that knowledge creates the theme.

Sometimes the theme is created by the events. 'Picking the right stocks' would be a success, but if you relied on some kind of information, say a magazine, 'knowing the right industry information' would be a theme. Without that theme of industry information you wouldn't know what stocks to pick. Conversely, if you have failed at picking stocks, you would list 'lack of industry information' as the possible theme.

Now, with all of this in mind, let's develop our themes.

This can be tough, so I will give you an assist here. Since these are the general concepts we see from our successes, it might help to have examples of other people's themes:

Success Themes

Knowledge about the market
Knowledge about my competition
Good interpersonal skills
Great with technology
Good relationships with network
Great attorney and accountant
Forward looking planning

Having looked at this, open your workbook to page 9, Success Theme Free writing. The reason we will use free writing is that it's the fastest way to look at the successes and find themes by not over-thinking it. Here's a few a tips on how to get the most out of your success theme free writing.

-Use the exact same format you used for goals in terms of time.

-As you look through your goals you may want to group them together based on their nature, such as personal life, professional life, children and family, hobbies and interest.

-Ask yourself questions: What are you good at? What do you do well? What do you fall back on when it seems like something you have worked on may fail? Who are you familiar with and how do you know them? What have people always told you is a strength you have?

With the examples and guidance above in mind, free write on your success themes.

Success Theme Development

We now know success themes are your skills and personality traits that allow you to succeed. Do not worry with 'filled out paperwork on time' or 'went to gym every day.' Instead look at the successes you've listed and view them as parts of a story in a book to identify our success themes. These themes help us through the events, guiding us success to success, or causing failure after failure. As you list them on page 10, these should be general concepts you glean from your successes. Now, let's go back to our examples:

Success

Moved to bigger house
Tried new business ventures
Won sales team of the year
Bought new car
Learned how to use IPad
Traing for half marathon
Got $10,000 more in savings
Won Acme Co project
Started new blog
Gained 300 new instagram followers
Made successful network for blog
Ran two 5 K's
Project featured in industry magazine
Published my first article in magazine
Managed three successful team projects
Developed good attorney relationship
All three kids got straight A's

Success Themes

Knowledge about the market
Knowledge about my competition
Good interpersonal skills
Great with technology
Good relationships with network
Great attorney and accountant
Forward looking planning

In each of these themes we recognize the underlying details that made the individual events happen and find that a theme applied to more than one. For our example the person built a blog, became proficient with an IPad, and gained Instagram followers. That's being good with technology. In the successes listed the person won projects at work, especially the Acme sale and made enough money to add to their savings. So the focus should be on the reasons for these wins which may be 'I know a lot about the market and can make good predictions.' The 'knowledge about the market' is the theme that guided this. They published articles and built a network through their blog, which helped them find opportunities, so that would be 'good relationships with network' would be the theme. In this book we are using general descriptions and actions in these examples because everyone is different.

Failure Theme Development

This may be the toughest part of the entire process because you've got to dig deep into what about you caused your failures. These are the personal shortcomings that cause the failure. Unfortunately, we can't say 'I have great things about me that create a success theme, but failure...well that's just coincidence!' We don't get to have a superpower without a weakness. When you develop these failure themes it is no different than how you did successes. Just like successes, you must look at your skills and personality traits and see what about you created these failures.

Just like in successes I'm going to give you some examples to help you out with your free writing. Now, I could list out hundreds of failure theme types to help you, but if I did that this wouldn't be about you. A list of types would fit you to some template. You're not a template or a piece in a puzzle - you're you, an individual who's working toward success. I can't be there with you to do this, though you can go over to our website and see if people will help you out on the forum, or on our Facebook. As you develop these failure themes I want you to remember that what you are writing is the reason you fail, and fail a lot. As you look at your failures list look for the clue to why they happened.

Here are examples I've seen in the past:

Failures Themes
Front end failures
Health was not a priority (alcohol)
Didn't organize money well
Didn't organize time well
Took on too many projects

With this in mind, free write your failure themes on page 11.

When we look at the failures from the year we can see the themes that caused the failures. Losing money in product launches and investment from the outset is a theme of 'front end failures'. There is a reason that the product launch or investment didn't pan out in the beginning, perhaps because you didn't plan them well enough. The inability to save and not having money to invest is a theme of being disorganized with money.

The key to this exercise is to see the underlying theme behind failures. If someone planned to lose weight they would have to have a few goals they failed at. Losing the weight, working out more, eating right - these are the goals they would have failed at. What might the reasons and excuses be for these failures? Working too much, having no time, and losing weight is 'too tough'... lemme tell you, I've heard it all. Was it losing the weight that was the problem...or perhaps their health not being a priority might be the underlying reason behind these failures. If their health and losing weight it was a priority life would not have gotten in the way. They would have made life get out of the way had it been a priority! Failure themes force us to admit what in reality is wrong with us, finding the disease and not the symptom. While this is a tough exercise, the further you reach, the more successful you will be in the next exercise.

Why Themes

You're probably thinking, 'Ok Matt, I get it, why spend so much time on themes!!!' Many people list their successes and failures quickly because they were individual events easily remembered. But, how often do you remember the underlying reasons? Rarely. This is because we focus on the immediate event when we look back at a failure. This is why we want to spend a lot of time teasing out what the themes are, defining them, and discussing how to discover them. Themes show you it wasn't mere luck or chance that made us succeed (or fail).

Instead, themes reveal that these events happen because of something about you.

This is one of the most empowering realizations you can experience...that there is something about you that makes you successful (forget failure for a moment). Who you are, what you do, your personality, or what you know that causes your successes to occur. When you move away from thinking you ended up in the 'right place-right time', and instead realize that you created both the place and time, you can become unstoppable. Yes, I said it - unstoppable. You become like a superhero who can make happen what they want to happen because you can make a time and place occur.

When we look at the concept of undoing the past we are changing our relationship to it. We become *ok* with who we are now; the person the past has created. That past has a hold on us in many ways, from our psychology to our neurology, even our taste buds. You can't unmake this or go back in time. You have already experienced those events…the question becomes: are you experiencing those events over and over every day because you relive them in your new experience? We have to loosen the ties that bind us to the past and our failures from the past…and our memories of these failures. When we see them as an event we can see what happened before and after, gain new insight into the 'why' of our actions instead of the 'what'. Severing this tie, undoing the past's hold on us, allows us a new approach to future events having learned from the past…and having let it go.

So use this exercise for more than just listing what you think may be a theme and instead look deeply into the concept…there is something about you and what you do that makes you successful and makes you fail. The point of this exercise is to search for that information and the underlying themes that made your successes possible.

I once led a business client through this exercise and some of those seated at the table were taken aback. 'Why are you forcing us to be hard on ourselves, we had a good year' was the reply I received. When we reviewed their lists we found that while there were more failures than successes, they only wanted to remember the successes. It would seem this is human nature, and for many it is.

But, there is a different path, one where we create our own nature. But, that's not planning, that's talking who we are as people.

The action of themes

Success is a pat on the back while failure is a kick in the pants. You remember the kick in the pants from the pain while the pat on the back is fleeting. Pain stays with you and the failures of the year might still bother you when you see them listed. I've found over the years that my failures per year far outweigh my successes but are rarely my focus. In today's world, failures are the focus for many. They gain sympathy in conversation with friends while giving those who do not like us a reason to talk about us. The success-to-failure ratio in this book's examples is equal to make a point...not to reflect reality. For every sale one wins, they might lose three. For every week we train for a 10K there may be three weeks something else was more important. With every successful business launch, five failed (I can attest to this personally!).

Every bit of information has to be thought about in these exercises and if possible you should go as detailed as you can down to the project name you lost. Even the name of the company you failed to launch successfully should be named because, in terms of marketing, the name means a lot. Remember, there is nothing wrong with failure, as Edison said, it shows us all of the ways not to do something before we get it right. Remember the whole 'individual event' concept? When we see failures as individual we recognize we have the power to stop them if we find the themes behind them and address failure from that angle.

Themes create a true picture of yourself and who you are: your strengths and weaknesses. I often tell students, 'Only you look in your mirror'. Your successes and failures are events you experience and live through. You develop memories around these events, and as we will discuss in other books at Pastless, your brain remembers it all in a very particular way. But, when events start happening repeatedly such as 'not enough time in the day' or 'being bad with money' this is more than an individual event. These are themes in our lives we have to address. Theme choice is a process that is more accurate than day-to-day successes or failure listings. It shows you the direct reflection of who you are day-to-day, event to event, not the day itself or the event as it occurred.

On page 12, write out the failure themes you see in your free writing, using our example is need be.

Take a look at your free writing and look for more concise ways of rephrasing them into bite-size portions like those above. If you have 'I am unorganized and that causes me a lot of problems at work' then you want to break it down to its simplest form: didn't organize time well. If you have money problems and you write 'I don't do a good job tracking my finances and it's messing up my credit report' then make it concise, 'didn't organize money well.' Your credit report is a symptom and I am sure there are other symptoms. Get to the core of the failures when you create your themes on page 12.

Here's a little tip that might help you if you are having a hard time finding your themes: investigate your successes and failures from a third party's perspective to find the theme. Think of you from the point of view of a teacher from the past or a boss you once had. What would they see that you might miss? What would your father see? What have people always told you? You might even call people you trust up and ask them to be candid with you! If people always say you were bad at time management and you see a list of things you didn't get done because you didn't have enough time...that should tell you something. If you were a fly on the wall between all of those individual events what would you see?

This process shows you have no one to blame or congratulate but yourself. You fail and succeed by your own doing. You may say, 'yea, but Matt, I don't have a crystal ball! I would've never seen some of this coming!' We will get to that and I'll show you a system on how to predict the future. But, for the moment, reflect and be honest with yourself. If you see in your failure list a particular theme, name it. If you don't know how to build the theme, contact me and we can figure out something because themes make planning possible. We can't plan event to event and be effective, nor can we fix our failures if we don't know what's actually causing them.

Phase 3: Correction

When I first began driving I would often confuse my brake foot for my accelerator foot. I would floor it when I wanted to brake, brake when I need to accelerate, and cause mayhem for everyone around me (sorry mom!). When the clutch was introduced this became even worse! The drivers around me avoided me and my passengers were suffering whiplash (sorry dad)! I smoothed it out eventually, going on long drives with my dad, and passed my first driving test. But, it wasn't until I figured out how to stop and go, then smoothly go, and drive in different places that I was able to take on the big challenge: a large U-Haul I rented to move across the country the first time.

Themes are like the brake and accelerator of the car we are driving. We can't get to life's waypoints, gas stations, rest stops, and end destinations if we can't learn to accelerate and brake. They work in unison, transferring energy, and ensuring we are always controlling our speed. To many people, success and failure would seem to be the accelerator and brake. One event doesn't make a person's entire day, nor does hitting the brake once make a bad driving experience. But think for a moment about someone with car troubles like soft brakes or a weak gas pedal. Their driving is radically different than that cars around them. Imagine further they have never known any other kind of car. If you put them into a luxury car with finely tuned pedals they would have a hard time driving and would take time to adjust.

That's what life after correcting your failure themes will be like…without the luxury car (sorry!).

Focus

Life can be like having soft brakes or a weak gas pedal: we work very hard driving and get little in return, and we never experience the joy of driving. Many people's lives are like driving a faulty car. They put constant pressure on the successes while ignoring what caused the failures. It's all they know and they focus only on success, missing out on a fulfilling life trying to solve individual past events. Many students of mine over the years looked at failures as a series of one-offs, and with enough of them, bad luck. Nothing could be farther from the truth! Failure and success might seem sporadic but eventually we draw to what we do best. Sometimes what we are best at (time management) causes success, and sometimes what we do worst (time management) causes failure. It's rare that a one-time mistake causes success or failure but in actuality a snowball effect of our themes in action that cause them.

If you have wondered why success seems so hard and failure seems so easy, there is good news. That good news is that within our themes we find our fixes. We can't move to a new year or new phase in our life unless we address our earlier failures and the themes that cause them. Our brains are not wired to 'move on' or 'get over it.' You can create a great plan but if you have fundamental failures that cause you to fall short consistently (which we identified in our themes) the plan will fall woefully short. So, we need to develop a self-correcting plan now to address these fundamental causes of failure that have been identified.

Often focus is put on our successes because of the immediate feedback they give our ego as they swell our pride. No one sits around the bar celebrating failure, though they should, it's a good thing because it helps us learn. With immediate feedback being the focus, we build on the success themes, and move past the failures quickly. Something important happens when we do this: we never learn from the failures. Yes, we might say, 'I'll never do that again' but instead of truly learning from it we focus instead on what we 'do best'. 'I'll never do that again' is avoiding failure, which is not the same as learning from it. Avoiding failure leads us to a life which is handicapped because we in time get by on our success themes which is only a percentage of our capability. This is living life halfway because when we change the traits that cause failure we can focus on our strengths. Our process leads to rarely worrying about our failures because they were fixed, or if they do pop up, we see them immediately and realize them for what they are: fixable.

To fix a failure theme is tough because these themes go to the deepest part of our personality and habits we might not even realize we have developed. But, while others get lost in a life lived by themes, in this book we are developing a map. Our success themes are a powerful tool in overcoming failure themes. We can overwrite our failure themes with new themes and habits, or overcome them with success themes. If we can find ways to apply our success theme to those themes that cause failure, we can create strengths from them.

How did I develop this? Well it comes from martial art and the term muscle memory.

My father used to tell me 'it takes 21 days to start a habit but a lifetime to break one' and while it's an interesting rule, it's not entirely accurate. But, it gives a glimpse into the apparent nature of what we are up against. As we've discovered, sometimes failures are a snowball that become a habit, like being late. Think about how many habits you will develop over a lifetime you don't even know that you have. Now think about breaking those habits. Until we looked at themes in this book you might not have even known they exist! How hopeless would that seem, trying and failing to fix individual events of the past that became a snowball? How many ways could you try to stop a bad habit during a lifetime? Just ask a smoker or someone who says 'uh' during conversation a lot if you want to find out how hard habits are to break.

So, instead, why not break the box and do something new in place of the habit?

Why not develop a new habit to replace the old habit?

Themes are patterns. They are one behavior repeated over and over until they make up an overall pattern of behavior. Being late, or procrastination, is done so many times it becomes your pattern. That pattern is the theme. It's something we do so often it becomes second nature whether it helps us or not. So, in our case, we can tell ourselves we'll be on time next time, or we can create a new way of living that ensures our being prompt. We substitute using a calendar and setting our watch back 10 minutes to create a new way of living. Instead of trying to change the pattern we generate a new one.

Does this make sense?

Make sure it does as this is one of the keys to changing yourself outside of this book. This key is called substitution because for our brain it's often easier to replace a habit than to change it. You begin something new as opposed to stopping what you are doing. You can't go back in time and change what you've done. If this were possible this book would be about building a better time machine and not a time changing machine called planning. In dieting you don't lose weight by eating less fatty foods...you change your food completely. If it's driving, you don't change the gas mileage on your car by changing how you drive your massive SUV, but instead you get a hybrid. If you try to change what you are doing, you'll never succeed when there's so many working pieces as we discuss at the previous link about muscle memory. Instead you must replace the pieces with something new...a new pattern...a new theme.

Keeping all of this in mind let's fix those failure themes!

Fixing failure themes

The best way to create the fix is to take each failure theme and create a process that will address it. Your question may be, 'Matt, will this solve the failures?' It depends on the answer to this question: is the failure theme a habit we've picked up; or is it deeply rooted psychological (depression), or chemically based (addiction)? If you've picked up a behavior like procrastination in living life, we can probably fix it. If a theme is a deep rooted psychological issue, or chemically based, probably not. We can create some new habits to mitigate the effects in this psychological or chemical situation. I firmly believe, because of how we are 'wired' neurological, that few failure themes picked up in living our lives day to day can't be negated by a new process that becomes a substitution.

So, take your workbook, your listing of successes, failures, and themes and let's develop a route to success

Starting on page 14 I added questions to help you. As you've written out your success themes and your failure themes, take a look at these questions. Failures and successes are usually interconnected with each other as well as other areas of our life. You would be surprised how many smokers I know with bad time management. This is usually because they have a brain and body not firing on all cylinders. It leads them to be slower over time physically from the wear and tear of smoking...and mentally because they sleep poorly. But, beyond this, successes can be affected by a failure theme, and failure themes are sometimes hidden by a reliance on success. So, check out the questions for some guidance in developing your themes.

Failure Theme Correction

In the workbook you will see two sets of lists on page 15, Failure Theme Correction. On the left side list your failure themes. On the right side you should think an action plan to correct the theme, or an action that replaces the failure theme with a new behavior. Below is a section for Notes. I have found over time it's best to let the creative juices flow, and if you have to begin switching papers to take notes, you can lose a thought. So, if you have a thought that enters your brain about an idea for an action, or a plan, but you think it needs to be developed further then scribble it down there.

In the below examples you'll find the purpose of those exercise.

Theme Correction

Failure Theme	Action Plan
Front end failures	Business plans for all new ventures (success theme)
Health not a priority (alcohol)	Schedule workouts/runs weekly; no drinks after __pm
Didn't organize money well	Better financial planning per month to build reserve
Poor time organization	Utilize new calendar system (success theme)
Too many projects	Weekly organizational hour

For each failure theme look for a process you can create that will be easy to stick to. This cannot be a momentary change but must be a lifestyle alteration. You gotta change the way you live! What you decide on has to be actionable every day, every time, no matter what. It should also be something that is trackable that you can put on a calendar if you need to. If it's trackable you can manage it, measure how often you were successful with it, and make decisions about how to alter it to be more effective. You should stay away from general concepts or ideas and instead focus on an actionable behavior you can take. This way you can review each week and see if you performed it. The great thing about themes is they are a self-realization. Once you realize it you'll always be able to notice when you are doing something that causes failure and can act quickly to stop doing it.

It may be possible to take a success theme and apply it to each failure theme for your action plan. In each of these examples above I want you to put yourself into the shoes of the person who wrote these themes and the action plan. Think about how you would solve it, what you can learn from the action plan. Let's break down the prior themes and their action plans and see what more can be learned and the ideas behind the action plans.

1. Front end failures for projects are common for entrepreneurs and project managers, but can relate to anyone in business. For me this one is personal and happened to me years ago. In today's internet-based business world many people launch businesses like throwing spaghetti against a wall. They hope something they try sticks but considering launches can run $1,000 or more to get started this becomes expensive and time consuming.

I once launched a new company I was sure would work, but I did little market research into it. I had some good ideas and I had a ready customer base from my past successful ventures. Unfortunately, I didn't investigate deep enough into whether I would have a customer pool that would expand beyond that base. After the launch I realized I wouldn't have enough content further than the product I had released unless I ate up time in my other ventures, which were successful and profitable. I relied on other people to fill in the content blanks, asking them to write for my new site and make products for the new shop. These were people with their own companies and products and they contributed little.

The last arrow into the heart of my new venture was a company I was hoping to piggyback had a change in management and was no longer willing to promote my venture and incorporate it into their own programs. I saw an opening, I took it, but I had learned ways not to launch a business and wasted months working on the project only to have it fail. Better than years, right?

So, to be candid, front end failures is a true failure theme I've experienced first-hand...a theme I solved with requiring myself to develop a business plan and to use various vetting methods on my ideas before investing money. Yes, a business plan and vetting process was used for this book!

2. Alcohol is often the unspoken enemy of success and this one comes straight from a good friend of mine I coached. Spending too much money on it, too many drinks too late, or too many drinks in general can make imbibing a liability. I'm the first to say much of my best writing and brainstorming has taken place after a glass of Jack Daniels. But, the line between productivity and activity can become a fine line when alcohol is involved. Alcohol often causes one to sleep in late or be sluggish in the morning which leaves hours on the clock that could have been used.

In this example, my friend decided that setting a time to stop drinking alcohol could end this failure theme. Many clients of mine think they must have a drink to unwind after a long day's work. Unfortunately, for many of us today, at the end of the work day we begin another kind of work: family or hobbies or a side-business. This can lead to needing another later drink to unwind. If you work late into the night, you might have a late night drink. I did years in the fitness and health industry, sometimes at the cutting edge of movement and health, so trust me when I say that the older you get, the more your metabolism slows down, and that late night drink can be a problem for a lot of reasons. Your health can suffer because of improper sleep patterns, no one likes waking up with a slight hangover or trying to manage not having a hangover. So, by setting a time at which he stopped having a drink he adjusted his work and sleep schedule around it. For this example, setting this time is a firm behavior that is trackable.

Question: What is something you do at night that leads to you have a sluggish start the next day? Do you stay up too late because of children, or perhaps you binge watch TV shows? How would you solve this theme?

3. Not enough money for investing in new projects is a common theme for any entrepreneur. Every venture, be it new business start-ups to existing businesses, looks for capital for projects. In a later chapter we will talk about the various forms of capital available to you and you'll find that money isn't always the answer. But, for many, it's the first answer they turn to. In this example, the person decides to block off a certain amount of money per month to build a reserve.

Financial planning is not the purpose of this book and there are many great books for learning financial planning. But, having extra money beyond living expenses to invest seems like common sense, therefore planning to save extra cash is a corrective action. In this example the amount of saving and the way you save is determined by you, though we will work through how to do this in a later chapter. The important part to remember is that it's a theme and they have chosen a behavior (money saved) that is trackable. This behavior can also help solve the earlier problem of front end failures. More capital means better chances of utilizing outlets, like advertising, ensuring you achieve a greater front end success.

Question: How could you save more every month to make sure you gain a reserve for an investment? What could you cut out, or cut back on, in your life to save more money?

4. Poor time management is the killer of productivity. Just because you are active doesn't mean you are productive. When we look back on the day before sleep sometimes we find we did a lot and got little productive work done. In this example you didn't managed your time well and this can happen for a variety of reasons. One of the most common reasons I have found is taking on too much, which often leads to one too many projects and then missing important deadlines.

Fortunately, in our examples of successes, you've got technology as a success theme and have become great with technology and using a planner. You decide that using technology for time management would be an action plan. Find a good technology you can use and make the decision to schedule your calendar for a weekly planning hour. If you are good with technology you may be able to schedule down to the day or hour to fix a failure theme by creating a habit.

Question: How often do you find yourself overwhelmed? Do you take on too many projects, or projects you aren't capable of handling? How could you use a success theme to fix this problem?

5. As you can see often times your failure themes are interconnected. But, if you don't list them out you'll never know. Too many projects to keep track of can quickly become overwhelming for anyone and lead to some projects not getting the attention they need. By creating a weekly schedule that has organizational hours (for example, Sunday and Wednesday) one can review all of their projects efficiently. You could use organization software or a calendar to see project progress. When you set aside time each week to review your projects you must set a time that is best for you and your lifestyle. One note here is to never put a review time at a time that might not be free. Create a review time when you know time will be free, even if it's right before you go to sleep or when you wake up and drink your first cup of coffee.

Question: What failure themes do you have that are interconnected? How often do you find one failure theme causes another?

Connect the dots
As you work through your workbook remember to look for themes that effect other themes. The interconnectedness of habits is often unseen until one uses a process like this one to

list them out. Suddenly our narrow focus on individual events becomes a wide view and our failures make sense. Failure themes rarely happen in a bubble and by solving one we can solve many others.

In closing, as we look to move beyond the last year and address the year, and life ahead, we must remember one thing: failure themes must be addressed decisively. As you put together your corrective action plan just remember it took you years to develop these themes. It took you thousands of times doing them and you won't undo them overnight! Fortunately, the moment you start doing something different you are taking a step in the right direction. Never, never, never get down on yourself about the past. You might not have realized why you failed because you didn't know about these themes. Now you realize them and there is no better time than now to correct them. Even if you don't finish this book at least you'll have figured this out.

You are who you are and you can't change that. You can only change who you will become by taking action now! Your future-self will thank you and your past-self won't matter as much. It'll become a memory that reminds you of how hard you've work instead of a way of living that makes you work harder not smarter. So now let's look at you in the future and start setting up our future having fixed the failure themes that might have robbed you of success!

Phase 4: Goals

Goal listing is simple though it may seem to be a daunting task. It can seem overwhelming to list out everything you want to achieve. If you *try* to list your goals you'll eventually fall short...you can't try, you have to *do*. In order to *do* we have to free ourselves from the state of trying which means expressing ourselves openly. It's time we go back to free writing.

The first thing to do is to free write the goals. Write everything that is a goal down. Learn to ride a horse? Write it down. Climb a mountain? List it. Double the amount of money in your savings? Learn wood-working? Be president? Didn't accomplished something you wanted to that you thought about last year? List it this year. Do standup at a comedy club? Write a book? It doesn't matter what your goals are, how big, or how small, you know what you want to achieve in the year ahead. In the past you might have written a few goals because you were limited by your previous process, or the reasons like 'not enough time' that you might have told yourself. Now you get to write it down freely because you can take your goals from dreams to reality.

Goal Free writing

On page 17 and 18 there are two pages for a purpose - for you to take up as much space as you need to write your goals! Perhaps you like free writing and are getting it easily. Over time I have had students that aren't so fortunate. If you are still having a tough time here's a few tips to make your free writing easier.

   - Our brains work and think differently throughout the day and our concerns vary depending on the time of day. When the day is fresh and new your goals may be one kind, but at night, after a long day, you may see your life differently.

- Free writing your goals in the morning, and then again in the evening, is sometimes the most effective means of goal listing.

- You might try free writing after breakfast, then at 1:00-1:30pm or after lunch, then 6:00-6:30pm or after dinner.

- You may keep a voice memo recorder with you during the day. For example, if you are driving, use a voice memo recorder to record your goals, then listen transcribe it later.

- Use mobile technology available to you. Voice-to-text on phones is a powerful tool you might use. If you are walking and you can't stop to list a goal, pull out your phone and text yourself. Add 'Self' to your contacts with your own phone number. Whenever you have a thought or a goal send a quick text to yourself and keep going on with your day (this goes for all ideas).

- Go to a place that inspires you and try listing your goals there. Go for a long walk for exercise and use your phone. Visit a museum and take your workbook with you. Sometimes getting outside is the best way to get the ideas flowing!

On pages 17 and 18 of your workbook make sure you spend time to fill out your goals. If you want to take a day or two, even a week, to do this, writing at different times of the day, feel free...but never remove a goal. You should only add goals as you free write.

When you are finished with free writing, transfer your free written goals to the Organized List on page 19. Once you have done this decide if you need to further refine your listed goals. If you feel you could refine the goals further, perhaps make them more exact, then do so in the Refined List. Remember, we do this just to make sure we fully grasp what we have written, that it is definable and understandable. I have found that any task we want to work on or overcome in our lives, constant refinement is needed. The distance between start and finish can sometimes be made double by detours we don't have to take. When we take a moment to refine what we are doing, making sure it is still our original goal, that moment can save us days in the long run. So, make your goals as specific as possible whenever you can.

Reality Check

With your goals listed it is now time to decide which goals you will set out to achieve. The point of the goal listing was not to be outlandish, but looking back, you might realize some things you can't do. For example, unless you've been involved in politics for years and the presidency is within reach I wouldn't recommend keeping 'become president' as a goal. Instead you might transition to something more local, such as 'become active in local politics' or 'become town councilwoman.' I had one client list 'be an astronaut' and I asked him, 'Are you more interested in becoming an astronaut or in space?' When he answered 'space' we decided to replace 'be an astronaut' with 'buy a telescope and take an astronomy class.' So, as you look back, if you think something is way too large or out of reach, look at what your reasons for listing the goal was (see, themes have multiple uses!).

The key to a reality check is not to let reality destroy your dreams but instead enable them. When reality is applied to dreams...dreams can be become reality. We have to scale our dreams and goals to be realistic so we can make them reality. While being an astronaut may be thrilling, for most people who love space buying a nice telescope and going to an astronomy class will be as satisfying...because they can achieve that. Find how you can satisfy the reason rather than the act, like switching 'be president' to 'become active in local politics.' Make your goals achievable by finding the reason behind them. Adding to the failures list this year should not be on your goal list so make sure your goals are realistic and achievable!

Many will still place goals in their planning sessions that are unobtainable and this is ok. It's why we've developed a reality check system to help you! Let me add something here because some may be offended by the word 'unobtainable'. The purpose of saying something is unobtainable is not to dissuade you from achieving your dreams. The purpose is to make sure that what you set out to achieve is something you can attain; a state of happiness you can obtain.

NWM

The reality check on your goals is to put it to a test of needs/wants/means (NWM). We have to define the difference between a need, which is a requirement in life, and a want, which is a desire. When these are defined properly then you can make decisions on which goals are more important than others. Means is a matter of ability. Never let means rob you of a dream but instead realize you may have to work harder to achieve the means to your end goal.

Take a look at your list of goals and ask yourself these three questions for everything you list:

Do I need to do this?

Is there something in your life that requires you doing this as a necessity? If you don't achieve it, will your life be worse off?

Do I want to do this?

How bad do you desire this goal? Is this something that is more important than everything else you've listed? Do you truly want to do this?

Do I have the means to do this?

Many will say, 'if you had all the money in the world, what would you do?' The reality is you probably don't, and means (as we'll discover in the next chapter) isn't always about money. So, ask yourself, do you have the ability to do this?

Some people have a tough time answering these questions. So, let's take examples and apply the test to each example.

1. Increase my savings

Need: If you listed it, then you probably think you don't have enough money under your mattress. So this is probably a good time to start doing something about that!

Want: Doing this will require saving and sacrifice, so balance that against your needs in life. If you have enough savings and there is something you've listed you want more, then you might not see this as a want.

Means: Can you afford to do it in your current living situation? Do you have a savings account? Is your savings account accessible and easy to put money into? If so, think about how you will accomplish it. Even if it's just a dollar a day, do you have the means?

2. Buy a Mercedes Benz

Need: Why would you need this vehicle? For work or for status? A realtor may need a nice car to drive around clients in, but someone who works for minimum wage may just need a car. Do you need the vehicle; does it help you in your life (which is not lifestyle)?

Want: How badly do you want a Mercedes Benz? Is this goal more of a 'want' than others? This is where need often comes into the picture, as you balance the want versus the need.

Means: Can you afford it? If you can, which Mercedes can you afford? A new one or an older one? What are you willing to give up to achieve this goal?

3. Climb a mountain

Need: Why do you need to climb a mountain? Was it a promise you made a loved one who passed, or a promise you made your 5-year-old self? Do you need to prove something to yourself or is this part of an endeavor that would make you money?

Want: Do you want to do it? Climbing a mountain requires a lot of equipment, which means sacrifice to afford it. Do you want it that badly as opposed to a car or savings?

Means: If you live near the mountains you've got the means to do this easier than someone who lives in a place where the nearest mountain is a 6-hour plane flight away. Being far away means flying and bringing your gear, or shipping it. Do the means exist?

Remember we are looking to make your goals attainable. No matter how bad you want some goals you may have other goals you need to accomplish. For some goals you will have better means to achieve than others. It's a matter of balanced give and take between your needs, wants, and means. When you find that balance you'll find you can switch between them, recognizing when you need change in your routine while still attaining the goals you set out to achieve in the first place.

Perform the NWM test

After looking back over your list and asking yourself these questions it's time to put pen to paper. First, transfer the organized goals from page 19 to page 20, refining them further if possible. This may seem tedious, silly even, but it's the only way to make sure you are constantly defining your goals! If you listed 'climb a mountain' as a goal you might refine it to name a mountain range when you transfer it. We refine our goals each time we transfer them to another page...so we can take another look and see if we can define them better. This is something you should always do.

After writing your goals down again circle the Need, Want, and Means next to the goal in your workbook. Be candid with yourself for each goal and focus on the NWM questions. If you are to be successful in the year ahead, you have to have reasonable goals or you'll give up. Be willing to say, 'I really want that but don't need it.' Secondly, you need to develop a balance of needs, wants, and means goals to keep you interested and happy. If you don't know the answer to the NWM questions, go research! You can always take time away from your NWM test if it means picking the right goals later. Go online and research the goals, talk a friend, go to the library, see what it takes to achieve items on your list.

Avoid doing this exercise in a vacuum! Compare goals to each other and see if one goal is of greater importance than another. If you have no savings and need more money in the bank then every goal may seem to be dependent on that. You may find related goals as you may write, where you listed 'new job' and 'more savings', and you can tie these two together in the next step in our process. You may find 'climb a mountain' and 'Mercedes Benz', where you have the means for both but have to decide which is more or a want or need.

Don't worry about deciding right now, just circle your Need, Want, and Means and get ready to move on to the next step.

Now, go back through your reality checked list, look at it, and recognize something:

THIS IS THE FUTURE-YOU TAKING SHAPE!

YOU'RE CREATING THE FUTURE!

IN 6 MONTHS, YOU WILL BE DOING WHAT YOU DECIDE RIGHT NOW!

IN 12 MONTHS YOU'LL BE LOOKING BACK ON YOUR SUCCESSES!

No more wondering or driving lost on the back roads of life...you're now driving a strong vehicle you've built! You know it's strengths and weaknesses. You've experienced its performance in good and bad areas. You know what it takes to make sure it works well regardless of weather.

Now you are setting your destination based on that vehicle, YOU, that you've developed.

So, get excited!!!!

This is the you that you want to be.

This is not past-you...the you that had dreams but 'life' got in the way. You are creating the person you will become - all of your hopes, dreams, and plans - put on a sheet of paper. By writing all of this down you are giving them a breath of life they may otherwise have not had. You are setting goals now so you can live each day to achieve them and the potential is endless if you make the decision to execute. A lot of books would stop there! They tell you to execute, to go and achieve the dreams you've listed...with no real plan to do so. That's not how we plan and it's not how billion dollar businesses plan. In our method we need to find the differences between all of these goals and find out what we know about these goals today.

Sun Tzu, the famous Chinese general, once wrote 'Victorious warriors win first and then go to war, while defeated warriors go to war first and then seek to win.' If you haven't read <u>The Art of War</u> I highly recommend you do. It may seem tedious to read at first but when you apply it to your own life, as we are doing now, you'll see it's filled with information you can use. Victorious warriors win first then go to battle because they list what they know before ever facing the enemy. So, if we are going to win first then go to battle we must learn what we know about ourselves.

Creating the future means planning for it and planning for it means looking at your failure themes. For a moment look at the failure themes, your action plan, and compare these to your goals. You know right now these stand in your way! Look for where these themes could affect you attaining your goals. Life happens with or without your consent - you can't stop time but you can make the most of it. Making the most of it means not repeating past failures in the future. By knowing your failure themes you can see which goals they would affect most. Chances are, if you prepare for these themes to happen you'll expect it when it does and you'll be able to deal with it.

The 5 W's

It's time to refine your goals again as you transfer goals from page 20 to 21. You might look at your NWM's and decide you could refine a goal a little further, so make sure you do. Once you have transferred your goals over we need to ask some questions about today. In this section we ask ourselves the who, what, when, where, and why. This is information that exists today about your goals. The 5W's gives us valuable information about our goals and help us decide what's achievable quickly versus those goals that will take more time to attain. After listing your goals again, and refining them, ask yourself the following questions.

Who
Who do I know currently involved in this goal? Who do I currently know who has achieved this goal? Who do I know that can teach me about this goal? Who can I partner with to achieve this goal? Who is an accessible source of information for this goal that I don't know personally I can access today?

What

What have I already done previously to get me close to achieving this goal? What do I know today about the industry this goal is in? What do I currently own required for this goal? What skills do I have currently that will help me achieve this goal? What do I currently own that will help me achieve this goal?

When

When are groups meeting that are related to this goal I can attend today? When can I work on this goal today and not take away from other things in my life? What are my strengths I have today that will make this goal achievable? What have I done in the past to achieve this goal? When do I need to start on this goal to achieve it this year?

Where

Where do I need to go to achieve this goal and do I have access to that area right now? Where is the most likely place I currently have I can work on this goal without distraction? Where can I find others today who are working on this goal? Where are clubs or websites I have access to today that I can use to achieve this goal?

Why

Why would achieving this goal assist me today? Why is this goal achievable for me? Why would I rather do one goal over this goal? Why is this goal more important than other goals?

Notice these questions are based upon today. This is done so that you can find out if you have the means to achieve the goal today. If you have a who, what, when, where, and why...this is going to factor very highly as opposed to a goal where you have one W, or none at all. As you ask yourself these kinds of questions, plus any you can think of, if you find that you have answered one of these questions...circle the corresponding W.

Phase 5: Divide & Conquer

One important aspect of planning is planning beyond one year into the future. I won't take a lot of time to discuss the future for two reasons. One you know the future is important. Two we have an entire book coming out on this so a lot of what will be in that book you'll be able to apply. Right now we have to think about something that may have been a thought 5 years ago but wasn't: planning. We have to look at the future and plan for it in an organized way. This requires an important thought exercise to think about who you will become after this planning period. It's time to have a conversation with someone you will meet one day but have no idea who it is today: future-you.

The question you need to ask yourself is: 'Who do I want to be in 5 years?'

5 Years

In the workbook on page 23 you'll find a series of questions to help you with your 5-year plan. This isn't an all-encompassing list and I encourage you to create your own questions or look online for other questions to ask yourself. The questions listed are the most direct I developed over using this process with business and individual clients. Like everything else in this book, the more direct and thoughtful you answer, the better understanding you will gain of where you want to go. You will want to stay away from general answers, using terms like, 'rich', but make it more direct. Who do you want to become? Look at your goals, see the themes within them. What do these goals say about you? Where do you feel yourself going versus where do you want to go?

When I first did this I had listed out a lot of goals, but when I asked myself 'Where do I want to be in 5 years' I found the categories lined up.

At the time I listed the following goals (notice how refined and specific the goals are):

Personal: live in a house with a larger garage

Business: find a job where I am valued in the industry

Finances: have a certain amount in the bank and three times as much in savings

Hobby: author 1 book that isn't martial art related and 4 articles in magazines

Who did I want to be in 5 Years: a successful, well-known author and speaker.

The Big Find

It was only after I listed my 5-year goal I saw how things began to align. I needed a large house to teach martial art at home and stop paying for gym fees, giving me more capital for other ventures. I needed a job I loved so I could enjoy my work and not focus so much on the day-to-day grind. This would give me more time to do the things I love to do outside of a job. I needed more money in the bank so if I had to go without a job for a period, I could. I had the *big find*, which is what I call something when you have a realization of what your true end-game is.

I wanted to break out of the martial art industry. My goal was to focus more on being an author and speaker than a fighter. I'm still working on that, but this book is part of that overall plan. I've been blessed and I thank God every day for the goals he's allowed me to attain. My life, through teaching, has been about giving back but I wanted to do more...to change more lives than I have already done around the world. There were a lot of goals but when I looked at where I wanted to be in 5 years, many paled compared to a book like this. I had listed more things, like 'buy a motorcycle' and 'go skydiving', but I had found who I should become and my goals listed above were creating the means to achieve that goal.

With this in mind, go back through your categories and make note of any goals that lead to your 5 year goals on page 24. I've added questions to assist you in the process. The result here is understanding some of what you are planning in the near future will affect your distant future. As we have all learned as we age, the distant future becomes immediate rather quickly! Like a car swerving in front of us, the future can seem to come out of nowhere. Taking this into account in our planning ensures that we have one eye on the distant future so we know exactly when it's coming because we have prepared the route to get there.

Divide and conquer your goals

A high quantity of goals can seem insurmountable while too few can lead to distraction because you don't have enough to keep you busy. You need to find a balance in living everyday life and achieving your goals. No one lives forever and tomorrow's goals becomes yesterday's 'I wish I would have…' As my uncle once told me, 'you never think you'll die until you do.' Time is the only currency in this world you spend and can't get back so we have to make the most of it. Few can make the most out of doing 100 things at once so we have to divide and conquer our goals. We've listed our goals and categorized, see them for what they are because of the information we've got…now, let's decide what we want to choose as our goals for the year.

Let's remember something important: we aren't setting goals to set goals.

This isn't an exercise to seem organized.

Pick goals based on first the best chance of achievement that are realistic and pass our NWM and 5W's tests. Secondly we look to goals that lead us to our 5-year goal. If we can tie them together, even better so we are in a better position in 5 years by acting today. Realize success and achieving goals means being selective about the tasks we say yes to. If we say yes to everything we decrease our chance of success at anything. Instead we have to have a willingness to say 'no' to the things we have little chance of attaining. When we say 'no' and understand why we are saying no, we can fully embrace saying 'yes' to the goals we've got the best likelihood of achieving.

So, in your workbook, let's finalize our list of goals for the year!

Category Based Goals

Categories are important and are the final step in our process. By dividing and conquering our goals we can find balance in what we want to achieve and how we will achieve them. Take time to fill out the Category Based Goal questions on pages 25-28. This will help you narrow some of your focus on your goals.

I based the Category Based Goal questions on what I have found other students have wanted out of their lives in planning sessions as well as commonly held goals people want to achieve in life. In Personal Goals, topics of happiness, bucket lists, travel, etc. In Business Goals look at your career, not a job, and answer common questions for those in the business world. Remember, whether you own your own business 24-7 or work for someone else 9-5...business goals can take up a lot of your life's minutes. Financial Goals are common for those wishing to get out of debt or make more money. My personal favorite, hobbies/interests, looks at your spare time, when you aren't working or with the family, and how you wish to propel your own personal potential through interesting pursuits. These questions are tough for some, easy for others, but it may help you decide if your goals are in-line with what many others have listed for their goals.

Almost done so keep up the energy...!

Need a break, take one!

We are coming to a close here and about to make our dreams reality

Our 4 Categories

Categories are the last line of refining our goals because it is a means of creating balance. In today's modern world balancing work, life, money, and interests is tough. If one area of your life is out of balance the others can quickly become unbalanced as well. Part of having achievable goals is having balanced goals. If someone has nothing but work goals and very few personal goals, the people around them in both areas of their life will suffer. 'All work, no play' makes us less likely to look back in 5 or 50 years and be proud of what we have accomplished in terms of what we achieved outside of work and business.

Personal
If it concerns a personal goal you've had, something you've always want to do or try, it goes here. The simple rule for this is if you think 'I want reflect on life when I'm 80 and say I did _x_' you should put it here. I've had friends and clients list personal goals under this category from 'spend more time with my children', 'see jimmy buffett', 'fix up a 69 Camaro' and 'ride a horse.' Sky's the limit here, and while you're at it – list sky diving!

Business
The simple rule is, if it involves a boss, even if you are the boss, it goes here. If it's regarding work, forming a business, finding a job, etc., it should go in this category. No, your significant other does not qualify as a boss (see personal for that!). I've had clients list a variety of goals in the business

category from 'change departments' to 'create my own department', even 'start an online business selling wood carvings.'

Finance

If it you are looking at money, savings, retirement, it goes here. The simple rule to use here is if it involves an account dealing with a bank or financial institution if goes here. 'More money to invest', 'find new broker', 'put $10,000 in my savings account', and 'develop and stick with a monthly budget' are some of the goals I've seen listed in finance.

Hobby

Listing something as a hobby is an interest you want to do because you are curious or something you think you could become good at, it goes here. The simple rule here is if you always wanted to learn it, you should put it here. Learn it and do it are two different things. 'Learn to ride a horse' is a personal goal and 'become a horse riding competitor' is a hobby. If you list climbing a mountain that's not the same as becoming a mountain climber. Looking back when you're 80 and saying, 'I want to climb Everest and I did' is not the same as saying 'I climbed Everest, Kilimanjaro, and Denali with a group of people I met in a mountain climbing club.' Personal goals don't have clubs usually – hobbies do. So, list those goals that are hobbies you wanted to learn to do in your spare time. Hobbies are not permanent. You can change hobbies whereas changing your job or the amount of money you make is more difficult. In a lot of ways our hobbies and interests can be a space for creativity because it's not difficult to switch hobby to hobby.

Now, take a moment to refine any goals you need to refine and then transfer them to their appropriate category on page 29

Remember to be specific with your goals and their categories. If you can't decide which category a goal should be then refine the goal further until it fits into a category. We want to leave no stone unturned in this process and refine our goals down as much as possible. You shouldn't list a goal in multiple categories...when you blend them you can't track them later, and if you can't track them, measuring them is nearly impossible. This is why we need to be very specific. Make the tough choice between categories but no sharing or blending categories so you retain balance.

You may be wondering, 'what if I have too many goals in one category, and too few in another?'

Our purpose is to achieve goals...not just create them. Downsizing the number in one category while you add a smaller goal in another is completely within reason if you feel unbalanced. Completely removing goals at this point is reasonable, too. It's your life, your decision, so decide to make the decision! Remember as you make the decision to keep balance in mind. One large goal in the work category and three small goals in the finance area is equitable whereas 10 small hobby goals and 1 small goal in business may not be. Perhaps you have to spend the year traveling for work so you have a lot of work goals...just make sure you have goals to achieve in your personal life when you aren't traveling. You may feel confident in your career and need to focus on finances and a particular hobby. If you have 6 in one category and 2 in another you may want to begin rearranging, or removing goals completely. Just remember - balance.

Total Goal Organization (TGO)

We've come to the big time! You might read all of this in your best monster-truck sportscast announcer voice! By the way, did you know reading aloud increases retention and overall personal confidence? Try it out, read these sentences aloud. Now we get to see our capability to achieve a goal. In your goal categories you should have a variety of goals written out. In TGO we look at whether a goal is quickly achievable or will take some time.

60

First, why do we call it TGO?

Anytime you set a goal, whether it's listed in your planning process or you are given a task at work, you should apply the TGO process to it. List it, then put it to the TGO process...needs, wants, means, who, what, when, where, why, and future-you. This will give you instant access to the knowledge you need to organize the goal. In our case, with this book and workbook, we will focus on the goals you've listed. So, once again, time to transfer. Take your information from page 20, 21, and 24, make any refinements you need to make, and transfer one final time to page 30. I recommend transferring it based on the goals with the most data points on down. So, if you have N, W, M, 5W's, and a 5 - list it first, versus a goal with just an M and 5. You might print out another sheet and rearrange them from most attainable to least if need be.

Now look at your goals and recognize there are some of these goals based on the TGO that you might be able to attain this week, maybe even today! This process is about attainability. Setting goals you can't attain will lead to being distracted by the day-to-day events of life, or losing sight of your goals completely. The small things in life become big things and take up all of your time if you have no achievable goals. When we set attainable goals we set ourselves up for success.

After you've done the transfer ask yourself if you are sure these are your goals? Can you commit to these goals? Are you missing something or is there anything you wish to add? We're coming to the end of the process so it's best to take a look now and make sure you want to achieve this list. If you aren't sold on the list you might end up skipping goals or thinking, 'well, I never really wanted to that any way.' Instead, you want this list of goals to be non-negotiable. Be sold on this list, knowing you can commit to this and if you achieve even 50% of the goals you'll be a more fulfilled person at the end of the year than you are today.

Ok with the list?

Is your success non-negotiable?

Is becoming better in the future more important than today's tedious tasks?

If you answered yes, then let's achieve them with a workable plan.

Phase 6: Prepare

We've had a harrowing journey in this book. I know because I do it every year and it's not easy. It's tough to look at yourself critically when in today's world easy success is within the stroke of a key or tap of a phone screen. But, you persevered! Be proud! We didn't grab a piece of paper and just list a bunch of things we wanted to do, put it on social media, then do only one. We went through the most thorough process you've probably ever seen to get to where you are now. Good for you!!!!! Successful companies are successful because they plan this way (and if you own a company you might decide to use this process with your team each year). When you get to 20,000 employees and billions of dollars you have to be thorough, critical, and honest. They say you can't put a price on health or happiness so why should you, with your health and potential, be different from a major corporation? You are your own enterprise and future-you is worth the work. No one ever puts 'not follow through' in their goals, but the question becomes: how do we execute with so much to do?

Preparation 1: I will...

First, we have to change our mindset so we will focus on declarative statements and use page 32 as a start.

As you fill out the Declarative Statements think about the work you have done so far. Our words translate our minds. When we use declarative statements, such as 'I will' we translate a mind that is forward thinking into words. Using words like 'I might' or 'I could' we link back to the past and the failure themes. Those phrases are the first things that have to go! Start to think of things in the future tense and when you are confronted with a problem refer to it like it is already solved. Replace 'I have to drop off the kids at practice, then I can meet up with you' with 'after I drop the kids off at practice I will meet up with you.' Future tense can be difficult but it will help you in many ways, from you believing you can do something to others believing you will do it.

When you look at what must be done as having already been accomplished you change your speech to be declarative and future focused to match your world-view. Many times it's not wanting, not willing, but deciding to make the decision before you ever have to do something that makes it a success. You always have a choice, even if it's a choice between the lesser of two evils, it's still a choice. Sometimes you can decide not to decide, and that's ok too, so long as you made a conscious decision based on the what you know.

If you repeat a phrase enough times you'll believe it which is why we have the declarative statements page. We often verbalize our psychology to our own detriment. I had a client who, through the entire process, kept saying 'this is so much, so in depth.' As the process went further he began saying, 'I don't know if I can do all this.' I advised him to reduce the number of goals if he felt overwhelmed because he could always come back. But he wanted to make it through to the end. After we finished we went our separate ways and within three months he had already fallen off of his plan. When I quizzed him about what happened he said, 'it became so much, I kept turning off my alarms so I could handle day-to-day issues.' It didn't become...it always was.

Upon further reflection and conversation this individual turned out to be less interested in personal transformation and more interested in going through the process to tell others they had done it. Not good! You need to be ready to embrace change, not just hug it. Declarative statements help you do this...they verbalize your psychology. With this in mind don't just write it down - say it, and if you have to pull this page out every day and read it aloud, do it. Now fill out page 32 and truly believe what you write!

Preparation 2: Capital

You're probably wondering, 'How the heck am I gonna do all of this????'

Over the years I have had friends and clients tell me about projects they were starting. I would always hear a few common statements usually combined with: 'I wish I had an investor' and 'This would be so much easier with an investor'. If you look at you as a startup you're going to need capital which is why we are going to look in depth at the capital available to you.

If we are to carry out our plans, achieve our goals, we first want to determine if we need capital. Whether it's picking up a new hobby or growing your business, there are a few kinds of capital at your disposal. We often think of wealth when we think of capital, then we think in terms of money, and our goals resemble 'make more money' so we don't need to ask for it. Capital is money or assets owned by a person or organization that can be used for a particular purpose. When people tell me they wish they had an investor to throw capital at their projects I often to tell them, 'You are your own capital'. You have the time to spend, your own money, you even have employees i.e. friends you can ask to help you.

Goals need capital. You won't grow your success without it. But, remember the definition is money OR assets. When you shift the way you view the concept of capital you find it is readily available. This may seem strange and to some they may say, 'so, like an investment?'

No.

Let's do some economics 101 here so we are communicating at the same level. Money is a thing of value you trade for goods and services. Currency is a thing used as money. There are many forms of currency, from dollars to Bitcoins to silver, all of which are traded for goods and services. You need money (something of value you can trade) for capital, which means you need a form of currency to use as money. Step back from the concept of what you think of as 'capital' and 'investment' for a moment. Forget that it's 'money' and instead of think of it as currency. Currency takes many forms…. your time, people you know and their time, their connections, etc., are all forms of currency you can use to provide capital for your dreams. This is why we earlier did the 5W's exercise: so we could begin to develop capital without dipping in our own pockets.

In achieving our dreams there are various types of capital: financial, human, social media, time.

Financial Capital

One simple way to think of capital is money not spent on the essentials. If there is $20 in your pocket and it's not being used for life's necessities (purposes like room, board, food) …you have $20 in capital. If $18 of that $20 is reserved for those other purposes that's only $2 of capital. But, it's $2 you can use for something. You can buy a calendar for $4 or have a website for $8 a month. I don't know your individual circumstance so I can't tell you how to spend or save. But, I can tell you that $20 or $2, if you don't spend it 'wisely' it may as well not exist. In my mind, spending it on your goals and future is spending it 'wisely'. So, look at your goals and your budget, take stock of what you have. Make a decision on how much financial capital you need and then adjust your budget to fit your goals after caring for your everyday needs. If you find you lack money to achieve your goals…start making changes so you do. Then allocate your financial capital according to what you have versus your goals. If you have goals you can achieve on $2, achieve them first before bigger goals, then save more money for the next goal. Divide and conquer. Remember we are in the business of achieving goals, not listing them. Besides, 'read a book a week' as a goal costs nothing when you have a library card and you'll still get the satisfaction of achieving that goal.

This book is not only a process but also my advice so let me give you some. Goals can be achieved on a shoestring budget. As you'll see in this section of the book you might not even need financial capital to achieve your goals. That being said, many times people feel they must hire someone to help them achieve their goal and that someone they hire becomes a big expenditure. Over the years I looked at what work I could pay someone versus the time it would take for me to learn to do it myself. If I have the time I take a class and do it myself. Obviously on occasion people must be hired, so I spend my capital on hiring someone if I am out of my depth. But, if I know how it is done and but I have no time to do it myself, I can make sure it's done right and on time due to my understanding of the task. This understanding saves me money in managing someone so they don't waste time doing the project I hired them to do. At this point I can build websites, run online shops, graphic design, film and edit professional quality videos, professional photography, and a host of other skills (I call them talents!) I've learned. Even if you only know the basics, remember those basic skills may get you through a project instead of hiring someone to do it from the outset.

My advice is when you have financial capital spend it on your own knowledge first before ever looking to hire someone else. Set aside an hour a day and learn something new. Eight hours for an online class may be $150, but you'll be glad you did it when you didn't need to hire someone that is $50 an hour for 8 hours. After you've gone as far as you can with your skills hire someone to finish your work for you. It's your money, not theirs, so gain enough knowledge to have the capability to manage the people you hire.

With this in mind, fill in the questions on page 33.

Human Capital.

The people you know, or the people you can pay, are forms of capital but often we think of 'human resources'. This kind of capital is not about managing lots of people and their benefits but more about making good use of the people you know and increasing your network. There are plenty of networking books so I won't bore you with networking advice. For human capital, if you can ask a favor, trade or barter, or (as a last resort) pay someone to do a task for you - you have human capital. It can be awe-inspiring what people working together through innovation without financial capital can accomplish if they all buy into each other's dreams. Sometimes all you need to do is ask friends to help so figure out what you need done, and instead of asking everyone to help, ask certain people to do certain things.

People are more likely to perform a particular task they are asked to do, such as reposting an article you've written, than to repost every article you write as a campaign. 'Smart asking' as I like to call it, goes a long way and ensures no one says 'don't waste my time.' Ask them for a specific request at a specific time and nothing more. Other times you may use Craigslist to find someone to assist you when you don't know who to ask. I own a few cars and save thousands a year by using a mobile mechanic from Craigslist. He tells me the items to buy for repairs, I buy them, and he only charges labor or we barter. I also use sites like 99Designs.com, where I can leverage large numbers of designers for a project, and Odesk.com for bids on website work I need instead of hiring a full time webmaster.

Human capital means finding the right people to do particular tasks a particular way and nothing more. If you are over-burdening people with requests you will take up their precious time or they may feel taken advantage of. Instead, ask people for specific things by a specific date and once done, always...always...I cannot stress this enough in terms of human capital...always say 'thank you' ask if they need your help in return.

Keeping this in mind, fill in the questions on page 33

Social Media

Social media is a powerful tool for multiplying your efforts. The ability to reach large numbers of people quickly has revolutionized the world. The problem is that anyone can reach large numbers of people quickly...and spam their email addresses. Like a window filled with spider webs, dog nose smudges, and assorted amounts of dirt, social media can be tough to see through. To cut through all of this you have to find who to communicate with and what they want to be communicated with about. You most likely found this book due to social media because someone you know, be it a friend or Google, brought you to our site. But, we had to communicate with you something you needed so you'd pay attention to us in social media.

When you pull together financial capital and human capital...that's a powerful set of tools! If you have products to sell, social media is a large equalizer. You can also use it to save yourself time. If you're looking to take a trip you might ask around on social media and let others help you find what might take you days to research. Be direct in your messaging and remember the human capital axiom: don't waste my time. Communication is the difference between 'fire' and 'there's a fire in the back-office, I need a fire extinguisher.' One causes noise, one cuts through noise. Make sure when you use social media capital you cut through the noise, not add to it. Remember 'likes' don't equal purchases, they have to be combined with 'conversions' where you convert that like or share into a purchase. A recent study showed that the average number of followers per user on a popular app for photographs is around 800. The exposure rate of a photo is around 10%, which means 10% of your followers see what you post. That's 80. The conversion rate after this was 4%, so around 3. Being generous we can say 4. This is a wildly popular app that many businesses are beginning to utilize because it's very active, but in terms of these statistics, it's not very productive. So read up on how to best maximize your social media capital and use it efficiently then fill out page 34.

The greatest kind of capital: Time.

Remember that time is the one currency you can spend that you can't make back. We can see the effects of a 'I need it now' world in the number of firms who will do everything for you. I know a few who are a last resort when I can't do it myself. I have saved myself more capital learning to do things myself than I can ever count primarily because I saved myself time. When you are working toward your goals your most valuable capital is the time you can spend on the goal. There are only so many hours in a day and we all get stressed. So, looking back at your goals, you might look at skills you want to learn and add those skills into your goals. The more you can do yourself, or the more you can do to get you to the halfway mark and then hire someone to get you the rest of the way. This means more time for other goals!

You should generally look at how many hours someone would work on a project and ask yourself if you have that many hours to learn the skill they will be using. If you have the time, or you think you will have a good return on investment by spending the time, learn it and try it. You only have so much financial, human, and social media capital to spare at one time.

There is a theme in the world today of 'life hacks' and a method of hiring out your work through a variety of means. Just remember, this is easy for people with a lot of money. For those with less, money the money we do have spreads thin quickly. People acting as human capital will only help you so many times, and social media will only get you so far. So learning it yourself may seem to slow your timetable of achieving your goal now, but the future will be a different story. When you are able to do the work yourself and you have more financial, human, social media capital, and you'll be glad you spent time capital today to learn the skill. My advice is become more DIY (Do It Yourself) than SEDI (Someone Else Do It). When someone asks me, 'who did you hire to do that' and I answer 'me', I have achieved a goal that is hard to put a price tag on: self-confidence.

Now, thinking about this information, fill in the questions on page 34.

Combining capital

These are four kinds of capital you have access to right now that can be effective ways of advancing your strategy or ideas. Let's look at an example. You want to use social media to promote your product but you're not sure how. Many people would say, 'hire a firm', which is an option, but just remember: since you don't know how to do it yourself, the next time you need to promote a product, you will need to hire another firm. Or, worse, you could be taken advantage of by a firm telling you untrue information and billing more hours than they should. In time, if you aren't careful, a lot of your financial capital will go into operating expenses, i.e., hiring firms.

Instead, turn to your human capital. Remember those 5W's!

Who do you know running a successful business online and ask them. Will they teach you in exchange for your product? If not, how did they learn? Can you take a class, learn the basics, then show them your plan you have and get their feedback? Without hiring a firm, you've used social media to contact the person, used time capital to learn it yourself, and used human capital in having them looking over our plan. Combining capital forms is the ultimate business equalizer if you decide to do it.

Organizing your capital

Now that we realize the types of capital at our disposal, how do we organize them?

You should prioritize how you will engage your capital in terms of:

1) How much capital do you have?

2) How much are you willing to task?

3) What capital serves the project best?

How much capital do you have? Not how much money, but what currency do you have?

You have people...who do you know? How well do you know them?

You've got multipliers...are you on social media?

Are you good with writing, or filming on camera, or with photography? The difference between the three is the answer of blogging (writing), YouTube (filming), or maybe Instagram (photography). Think about what you have access to in capital. In this book we will help you make the list of goals but your capital is individual. Until you understand your capital you can't fully realize your capabilities for success. Often asking 'how much' and 'what kind' can give you insight into your capital. I often ask the following two questions to discover the best route to efficiency:

How much are you willing to task?

This is an important question. Once you understand the kinds and amounts of capital you own you can better task that capital in achieving your goals. Experience is a teacher...but success leaves clues. Look around at your competition and friends and see what they are doing well. If you have an opportunity no one has taken advantage of and a large amount of capital in one area, you may take everything you've got and throw it at the opening in the market. But, more often, you must be balanced in your approach and be willing to do some of the work yourself.

What capital serves the project best?

Deciding what capital best serves the project is easier than you may believe. The opportunity dictates use of capital. If you are balanced, then you saved a percentage of each check for use as financial capital and grown your personal and business network. You've created a social media presence that consistently grows without a lot of work (remember, time is the ultimate capital). You're ready to achieve your goals and use your capital to do it.

The effective use of capital lies in 'red lines'. Do you know your 'red lines' on when to pull back or push forward, or just to maintain? Success is often defined by knowing if you aren't seeing the results you want. at what point will you pull back? If you can't pull back and stop, or maybe just pause, you will soon have little capital left. Always have an awareness of what that point is and you set it before you ever get started. When you don't know where that line is, read what others are saying they do. Contact us for consulting, read articles out there, ask a friend or social media network.

Switching gears

Another part of effectively managing your capital is knowing when to switch 'capital gears.' Driving is an exercise in changing gears but often we forget the transmission is doing a lot of work to move the gears up and down. In most cars you can't stay in 1st gear and get to 80 MPH but many times people view business as the opposite of their car's 1st gear. I have had many clients and friends use one kind of capital to its fullest when they could multiply its effect by switching to another form of capital. Capital is limited and opportunities can require more than you've got, at which point you must switch to another form. Realizing when to change from time to financial, social media to human is a sliding scale that takes time to get a 'feel' for. You need history and experience, or to use your human or social media capital to ask, or your time to research and learn.

I once took out a year's worth of advertising in magazine, tied up a year of advertising money, only to track it and find I lost money. I used coupon codes in the ads to see what response I was getting. I even hired a designer to finish an ad I started. But, I didn't research the demographics and the shifts going on in the print market. I told myself 'this is a magazine everyone in this industry reads so of course the ad will work.' Of course, right, because everyone else is doing it, just like the 4% conversion rate above! It was active, so it must work! What I didn't realize was the level at which consumers were going toward online magazines instead of print media. With my financial capital for advertising tied up month to month I bartered training with friends who had stronger social media presences than I did. They would promote my work or we would teach in videos together. In doing so, I grew my social media capital while my advertising capital was contractually tied up. What I didn't do was pull from my operational capital to make up the balance. I needed equipment for better classes so I had to find a way around my advertising budget being sapped. I had to switch gears...I had no choice, and because I recognized my kinds of capitals, I was able to be successful.

In your workbook fill out the Capital Organization section on pages 34 and 35. You now have some ideas on what capital you have access to so use the questions to put them into play. When you understand your capital you can build an effective strategy. You can determine how to be successful and develop a team around your capital. Keep this in mind as you move forward implementing a strategy to achieve your goals.

Go back to your goals listed in the TGO. Look back at the 5W's and the forms of capital you have available. Between financial, time, people, and social media think about what kind of capital would you put toward these goals? Are there particular goals where there is lot of capital to expend, while others you have a limited supply?

Keep this in mind because now we are going to implement our goals.

The Process

If you do this whole process but don't follow through day-to-day, you're giving a side hug to your life...! You've 'friend-zoned' your future! If you want change you've got to bear hug this process and hold on for dear life to your plan. Otherwise you'll be wishing you had next year and going through this all over again...listing failures instead of successes.

So, before we get going with the easiest part, but the part that will challenge you the most, remember a few things:

1)Don't confuse the process for the results. As we move into implementation you'll see that each day you are moving toward your goals and it can be monotonous. Saying the ABC's seemed very monotonous until you could read basic words and sentences. Basic sentences seemed boring until you were reading pages. Pages seemed a little boring until you were reading books like this one. Being successful requires discipline, fighting the urge to skip the monotony, and embracing the process even when you lose sight of the objective. The process will keep you on track. Some days you're going to forget why you are doing a task...just do it, you'll be glad you did in the end.

2)Discipline doesn't delay. Discipline means that regardless of the situation you won't delay the action you need to take. This is the biggest challenge to planning success. A lot of books will give you a process to finding the 'new you' then leave implementation up to you. This is why we developed a process that does it for you. I am giving you a process in the workbook that made companies big dollars and we are developing future tools to help you more. Now you need the discipline to execute! Follow the path, don't delay, be decisive!

3)This should be fun! Seriously, this should be a blast! If success is your present to yourself, the process is the unwrapping. Remember the feeling of turning your goals into written word? When you see it on paper it's a different feeling. This whole process probably seemed weird until you got to a goal with an N, W, M, 5, and all 5W's. Then you realized, 'I can do this!' You finally realized you were on the path. Coming up, each time you execute, be it a reminder or review session, remember that feeling: you can do this, you can be a new you.

Prepared?

Let's do this!

Phase 7: Implement

The easiest and hardest part of planning is implementing the plan. You can plan until you have every moment of the day reserved for an activity, but if you don't do the activity, what's the point? Few plan to not follow through but unfortunately most people end up not following through far too often. You have a well thought out list of goals that are achievable but now we have to set ourselves up for success with some preparation.

First, breathe a sigh of relief: we will not be planning out an entire year, only six months. A mentor of mine once told me that while on a flight to vacation from New York to Hawaii he went to the cockpit mid-flight (this was pre-9/11) and talked to the pilots. The pilots told him that the plane was on autopilot on much of the flight and that they were only there to adjust it a little bit as they flew. That little bit kept it on course and if they didn't make the small adjustments they would end up in the middle of nowhere. It was the small adjustments that got it to its destination. Years later a pilot friend told me that wasn't exactly true but the sentiment is valuable. For us, in planning, we will be doing something similar in making small adjustments along the way to keep on track.

So, first, let's get our flight plotted with our list so we can set the autopilot.

Creating your map

If you're going to be successful in achieving your goals, you must develop an understanding of what it takes to achieve the goals. Think about driving your car with and without GPS in a new town. You can quickly become reliant on the GPS to give you turn-by-turn directions but if the phone dies...you're lost. You would need to do something my father taught me how to do: use a map. Traveling salesmen are famous for their maps and my father and his father were not exceptions. Both traveled the country selling different products but had extensive maps and road atlases. When I first saw my father's maps I was in awe. He had written on them notating points of interest, short cuts that didn't work, and restaurants for different foods. He was Google Maps before there was Google Maps!

While GPS gives us turn-by-turn directions, a map gives us the overhead view we can use to plan before the GPS tells us to turn. The road to success is similar. If you rely on GPS waypoints but you never pull out the map to get a general idea, you could end up lost. The planning we've done; the decisions we've made on goals...these are our map. Now we will create waypoints to let us know when we need to take the next exit or turn right on the highway of success.

You shouldn't have a large list of goals for the new year as you based it off NWM, 5W's, and your ideas about where you want to be in 5 years. The list that was large when you did the free writing is now narrowed and it is time to decide what steps to take to achieve the goal. If a journey of a thousand miles begins with one step, this journey begins with defining the route.

Hierarchy of Attainability

The Hierarchy of Attainability sounds complicated, but it's not. It's a regal sounding name for a way of making attainability easy to see. Taking the data from your TGO exercise on page 30, list your goals under their corresponding area on page 36. If you have a goal that has every criteria you'll want to list it as a 1, but from there we go through the hierarchy of attainability. As we transition to level 2, want no longer matters. Here we look at needs and means. The difference between level 1 and number 2 is desire. You may need to do something and desire to do it so you will attack it as hard as you can! But, if we remove the want and leave you with only needs and means, this may become a chore. Remember, balance! The desire may be wrapped up in the need and this is especially true when you are unhappy with something. Saving money, getting in shape, these are things no one 'wants' to do because they require discipline, versus a hobby like 'learn to surf' where you have a want and no practical need. I've been surfing twice, both times I was thrown back out of the water on to the shore and the ocean showed me what it thought of me, so I may be a little biased on surfing.

Pure want and the desire for something should not replace something you need to do. As we move down the hierarchy we keep a premium on routes to achievement, such as the means and 5W's. It is only at the end we come to no routes and no means. Now you may find yourself with something important to you, a need, being in level 6. You need to do it but you have no route to discovery and you might be thinking, 'but, Matt, I need to do this.' First, ask yourself, if you don't know the who, what, when, where, why - how badly do you need it? That being said, if this is still the case, then you should add gathering information *about* this goal as your goal, not the goal itself. You more than likely have the 5W's for finding out information. You can go to a library (where), talk to an expert on a forum (who), you can do it in your spare time (when), and your why is that you have a need with no 5W's, and you need the 5W's. At this point you might place 'gathering information about the goal' to your level 2 because it's a need and you have the 5W's.

After moving your goals over, refining if need be, take a look at levels 1 - 6. This will be the order of goals we will tackle as we plan out the next 6 months.

The Success Detective
This is where the rubber meets the road as you look at what you need to do to achieve your goal. On page 37 you will

find a lot of questions to help you make sense of the goals you've listed. You can print this page out for every one of your goals to organize them, but to start I would recommend starting with one goal from your Level 1 or 2 of the hierarchy.

Success isn't easy. Everything you know and can research is a clue leading you to success. Using the template list such as the one provided is a start to achieving your goal. As you fill out the Success Detective template write it all down. Don't hold back, go for it! If you don't know, research, ask someone, get a book, go to the web. This is where you start setting your waypoints for your map. Each piece of information you list will create your autopilot.

Becoming the detective and looking for clues often revolves around on how others achieved success. Get a spare sheet of paper and list out what you don't know. Use social media and the internet to research what steps others took on their route as well as the pitfalls they encountered. Use your human capital to tap the 5W's and list who would ask questions if you know people who took a similar path. Don't limit it to people who have been successful as they will tell you how they succeeded. Seek out people who previously failed in their trip and ask them what happened. It's never a comfortable conversation, but it's one you will want to attempt. Recently a friend of mine who was an angel investor wrote a blog about how he failed at it and why others shouldn't try it. He lost a lot of money investing, and while he recommended others not do it, his failures also taught a valuable lesson for those starting. I learned from his failures and followed up with him on the phone to make sure I understood the nature of his failure. As you research your goals look for the clues.

As you work to achieve goals, remember something: the tougher it becomes, the more likely you will be to switch to something that is easier to do. When you gather massive amounts of information and plan you make it easier. It's core of how we as humans act: we prefer easy and will repeat easy. Easy tasks bring easy success and success, even the smallest amount, gives a feeling of worth. But what kind of life would a life of easy success and no challenge or change be? We would chase that feeling of worth right now, distractions and all, rather than achieve our goals later. This is a reason many planning sessions fail: people get distracted by the day-to-day easy tasks.

Now, don't get me wrong, there is nothing wrong with easy. Proper preparation, like page 37, will make achieving your goal easy, but that doesn't mean your goal is easy. If achievement is too difficult you will be more likely to do something else. If you want to build a tree house from scratch for your kids, it won't be easy. But which way will make it easier to build the difficult dream? Taking the time and plan it out, perhaps ask a friend how they built theirs, get the right materials, asking for help and organizing your friends into a schedule...or just getting up one morning and trying to manufacture a treehouse with junk from the garage? One way makes a hard dream easier and the other makes it...well, makes the goal a bad, possibly dangerous idea. Sometimes the nature of 'easy' is not making mistakes you might've avoided had you done your homework about other's successes and failures. One approach is looking at how others achieved the goals you're looking to achieve and seeing if they have done anything that will make your route a little easier to navigate. Do this research and list these items down as well under your goals if you find them.

Goal Waypoints

You should now have a list of items with each goal from the template. Since I can't be there and help you right now we are going to go through an exercise to show you how to put all of this together. On page 38 you will see a sample of what we call Goal Waypoints. This is how we will set up the map.

On the Template sheet you listed your steps to achieve your goal. Some items you may not know the answer at this moment so you may need to make gaining that information a goal. Don't worry about listing information you don't know, list it as what you need to do to achieve the goal of gathering the information, and move on.

For our example in the workbook we'll say you have two goals. One is that you need to have $20,000 in the bank by the end of the year, and the second goal is to climb Everest one day because you want to be able to say you have done it. Which is more important? I'm gonna make a judgement call here and say obviously the money now and you make Everest 'one day' into a date 5 years into the future. After this you have your research and homework. You've figured out what you need to do this year to save $20,000 as well as work toward your 5-year plan. You've researched both goals and your research had led you to train, your list would look like this

Climb Everest

Need clothing

Decide what clothing should I buy first (Article I read said shoes)

Need gear

Should I get a backpack?

Should I get walking sticks?

Need to train - how much?

Where can I train locally?

List your 5Ws

Savings in the bank

Save money every month -

How much per month per week?

Do a budget?

How much do I need to save?

What can I cut back on?

How can I make extra money?

Hold a garage sale?

Drive for Uber?

List your 5W's

Now we create our sub-goals from the list above.

After you list a goal, begin to take the information you know and list it out as sub-goal. Under the sub-goal put anything you need to accomplish the sub-goal. Here we 'chunk it down' into doable items. If you are going to eat an elephant, you don't eat it all at once...you eat it one bite at a time! This seems like a lot if you have a small mouth, right? With your information, such as the NWM, 5W's, 5-year planning, and capital, you now have a bigger mouth to chew with. We are going to eat the elephant one bite at a time with a bigger mouth.

This is your general list of sub-goals to achieve your primary goal.

Start training to climb Everest in 2018

Buy shoes to train in

Make sure shoes are Salamon brand and above the ankle

Buy a backpack (really expensive)

Buy walking sticks

Buy Acme brand of walking sticks, but model for personal height

3 times a week, 2 hours a day on steep trail with gear

Be able to hike 3 miles in 1 hour on steep trail

Start with training plan (from website research)

Use an oxygen deprivation mask to simulate thin air (idea found on blog)

Find steep trails

Look up blogs for hiking in Maine

Have $20,000 in the bank

Currently have $2,000 in the bank

Save $1,500 a month

Cut back on going out

Only go out on Friday's

Switch to diet that is less expensive but very healthy

Cook at home and not order-in so much

Downsize apartment to save $200 a month in rent

Lease is up in April

Do not spend $1,000 bonus at Christmas

Will bonus be more this year?

Hold a garage sell

What is best way to advertise a garage sell

Joint garage sale

Janet has a garage of stuff - would she do one too?

So, this is our map and GPS beginning. You can free write this portion if you want. Interestingly you can see which goals will require a lot of time and effort. Perhaps down the road training for Everest will require similar effort to saving money. But, for now, that will be the bulk of the work it seems. But, with your finances on autopilot how much time will be left for goals like climbing Everest? A lot? This is the beauty of planning well. Before we get there we have to start putting together our GPS waypoints for our map. Now we truly chunk it down to achievable, measurable items we can track and know if we achieved.

Monthly Goals

Monthly goals are our big events that need to be achieved. It's important to remember there is only so much time and you've got a large list of goals, so you should work toward being organized. If we take the above example, then we would need to balance our other goals against this goal and see if there is something more important. So, we have goals listed...how do we decide on monthly goals? Many times our monthly goals are selected for us by their size and importance, or ease of attainability. We have to decide if we have time to achieve them in one month in terms of NWM, and our 5 W's. So, let's organize the list above. Take one goal at a time and list it for each month.

Climb Everest Sub-Goals

January

Buy shoes and walking sticks

Find steep trails in Maine

February

Buy pack back

Begin trying hiking plans

March

Test hiking plan progress

Find new plan to achieve goal (3 miles in 1 hour)

April

Start new program

Let's we add another goal, shall we...

January

Buy shoes and walking sticks

Find steep trails in Maine

Look at online forums, join a few

Research financial goal

New diet options for cooking at home

Cut back to going out Friday's only

Find new savings every month

Do monthly budget

Look at turning hobby into online business

End of the month planning day

February

Buy pack back

Begin hiking plan

Do monthly budget

Research downsizing apartment to save $300 a month

Garage Sale Research

How do people advertise garage sales?

Talk to Janet about garage sale

End of the month planning day

March

Test hiking plan

Do monthly budget

Find new plan to achieve goal (3 miles in 1 hour)

Finalize plans to move into new apartment

End of the month planning day

April

Start new program for hiking

Start preparing for move

Buy boxes, look at renting U Haul

Hold garage sale before the move

End of the month planning day

May

Move into new apartment

Find out if Christmas bonus will be the same as last year ($1000)

End of the month planning day

That came together fast, huh?

Popularly called 'chunk it down', in this process we have taken a large scale goal and made it smaller by dividing it into sub-goals to the first five months of the year. We've taken our sub-goals, our waypoints, and have begun putting them on the map. This is only two goals, you may have a lot more, but as we chunk it down more, it becomes manageable. The year starts busy, yes, but there is a reason for this. It's the beginning of the year and you are energized after your planning session. Your first month is generally the easiest part so research and setting up the rest of the plan. You might decide not to start working on a goal until late in the year and therefore not even list it. It's your decision, based on Needs, Wants, and Means. You may need to wait until there is $10,000 in the bank above before you can start another goal, or you may need to wait until later in the year to start your savings because you need to find a new job first. It's your decision and this process can't make the decision for you...it can only show you how to find what's important, what you can achieve, and a process for achieving. What you achieve and when is your business.

Weekly Goals

Now we go further down the rabbit hole of success and see how far we can divide and conquer our goals. Chunking it down further means dividing the month into the weeks of the month and deciding when you will get you will get to your waypoints.

So, for example, let's take the month of January:

January

Week 1

Buy shoes and walking sticks

Find steep trails in Maine

Look at online forums, join a few

Week 2

Research financial goal

New diet options for cooking at home

Cut back to going out Friday's only

Week 3

Find new savings every month

Do monthly budget

Week 4

Look at turning hobby into online business

End of the month planning day

January just got a lot easier looking, right? What was a large group of goals is getting smaller, more manageable.

Daily Goals

Don't you sometimes wish you could get more out of a day? You can by setting your daily goals. Daily goals are even easier but need a calendar and the discipline we discussed earlier. Rubber hits the road time! While we are developing some tools to help you with this down the road, no app or software is going to give you the discipline to answer alarms when they sound. You have to decide to make the decision to occasionally glance at the map to make sure you're on target. This is where our end of the month planning day session comes in handy because we can compare how we are doing with where we said we wished to be.

Let's take another look at January and add days. I have
added something important now that we have come to days.
I have set up every Sunday as a planning day. This should be
automatic, every week, so you can take time to reflect on the
week that past and the week ahead. You can look at your
map, see what you have and haven't accomplished or what
needs to be moved on different times and different days.

January

Week 1

Sunday: planning day

Monday: Buy shoes and walking sticks

Wednesday: Find steep trails in Maine

Thursday: Look at online forums, join a few

Week 2

Sunday: planning day

Monday: Research financial goal

Monday: New diet options for cooking at home

Wednesday: Cut back to going out Friday's only

Week 3

Sunday: planning day

Tuesday: Find new savings every month

Saturday: Do monthly budget

Week 4

Sunday: planning day

Wednesday: Look at turning hobby into online business

Thursday: End of the month planning day

In addition, as you add goals to March, you only need to pick days where you will do the goals.

Setting up the GPS

Daily goals are a matter of assigning a day for each of the weekly goals above. That's it! You set the goal in your calendar and on that day, at the time you set up, you do the activity that pops up on your calendar. You'll find as I looked at the list I made a couple of notes for myself as well, incorporating some of the W's that might exist, such as people to talk to and places to look.

<u>January</u>

Week 1

Sunday 9am: planning day

Monday 5pm: Buy shoes and walking sticks

Wednesday 8pm: Find steep trails in Maine - go look at Saddleback Mountain

Thursday 7pm: Look at online forums, join a few

Week 2

Sunday 9am: planning day

Monday 6pm: Research financial goal

Monday 8pm: New diet options for cooking at home

Wednesday 3pm: Cut back to going out Friday's only, plan weekend ahead

Week 3

Sunday 9am: planning day

Tuesday 11am: Find new savings every month

Saturday 1pm: Do monthly budget

Week 4

Sunday 9am: planning day

Wednesday 7pm: Look at turning hobby into online business - talk to Tom

Thursday 6pm: End of the month planning day

This is where technology is your friend.

Starting at the first month, week one of your planning, go through and start assigning dates and times to events. These are your waypoints for your success GPS. Start methodically assigning times each day in your calendar. I find this easier to do through a calendar you can link to your phone. You want the reminder to be instant so you can act instantly. Using a system like Google Calendar is easy because you can see the month on your PC, and then tie the Google calendar to your phone. If you don't like Google you can always find another system to suit you. Just remember to link it to whatever device, like a phone, you have with you all of the time.

One easy way to make sure you get the item done is to overestimate time. If it's an event that requires an hour of research, schedule an hour and a half. This way if you are doing something before and you run late, you can still get in your achievement time. If it's a call you think will take 5 minutes, put 15 minutes in the calendar so you can take your time, take notes, and make sure what you set time aside for is time well worth it.

Written calendars work well, but I sway toward using an electronic calendar. A few years ago I would have said either are equal, but the quantity of apps available today that can help with time and financial management...the written calendar can't keep up.

Now it's your turn.

Take it all and starting with goal one and start the whole process. What you will first find is why goals are rarely achieved. When you take a goal and break it down to what actually must be done to achieve it - it's a lot. Combine it with other goals, with everyday life, and distractions, and you find why people become overwhelmed. On top of this you'll find why most people never accomplish their goals: they never list out the parts that need to be done. You might find you had 40 goals before you began chunking it all down and you only end up with 10 left for the first 6 months of the year. That's great! It's better to have 10 achieved goals and then take on another 10 - than 40 you didn't achieve at all. Take a breath, dig into it, put it in your calendar and be proud. Pat yourself on the back...you have now set yourself up for success and have an autopilot to achieve your dreams.

Autopilot

When my mentor told me about his Hawaii flight story I chuckled, thinking of him in the cockpit, most likely telling the pilots how they could pilot better. But, over the years, the analogy made more and more sense as I planned my success. The calendar is your autopilot, now all you've got to do is respond to it and do what it asks. You today, when you are charged up and ready to succeed, are in actuality having a conversation with your future self when you set these waypoints. Future-self may be swayed by the day's events and you've got no idea what May Week 1 Monday will hold for you, but you can make sure that the feelings of that day don't affect November 1 when you need to have $18,000 in the bank. By setting your waypoints now, and letting yourself go on autopilot, you can do any number of things...but as long as you do what the calendar reminder asks, you can't fail at your goals without effort and self-sabotage.

On the road to successes, you need gas stations and rest stops. I am a big fan of rest stops and gas stations when I travel, especially if they have a view. The people, the stores, the interesting locally produced candies and treats sold at the calendar. I don't think there is anything better than an interesting gas station in the American southwest, except for a good highway marker and an incredible view. When traveling I often leave a little extra time for these kinds of places and have often found myself talking to a gas station attendant an hour after I pumped my gas.

Many times the journey is the destination as much as where we are trying to get to. When I first drove across country I decided I needed to delay plans I had at my destination just to take in more of the scenery and hear more stories as I traveled. I once lost one of my dogs in the desert overnight because I decided to camp out instead of hit a hotel. Was it frustrating? Of course. Did I get a great story out of it that involved scorpions? Yes. I would get home eventually, but the lessons I learned in the rest stops and gas station became as important to as getting home.

When you plan your goals out, down to the day, just remember something on that day, months later, when the alarm chimes reminding you: enjoy doing the task. That task is leading you somewhere and you can learn from it. Reflect on the prior tasks, look at your map, enjoy the journey. These are the moments you are getting gas in the car, as your reflection refills your energy.

Each week I recommend a 'gas station', which is a day where you pull over for an hour and take a look at the map. Reflect on your week past, look at what you accomplished, and see the week ahead and what you'll need to do to be successful. Do you need to rearrange the waypoints because of certain meetings, or travel, or perhaps your child has a doctor's appointment? There is nothing wrong with this, so long as you finish the tasks, the day isn't as important as the child's appointment. That's why we have the weekly gas station, to review our map and see if we need to adjust our route.

Each month you need what I called a 'rest stop', or a monthly planning session. This can be a day, or just a few hours during one day, where you take out the map and make sure you're on the right track. Look at everything you accomplished in the month before and reflect how much closer you are to your goals. You can also use the rest stop to refuel on events you missed. You might find an event you missed during a busy day or a forgot to go back and accomplish. You can use this day to get this waypoint covered and get back on the right track. Take a walk around the rest stop and look at the views, read the signs that are everything you've accomplished. When you walk around your personal rest stop you're able to get a sense of your small victories and the ground you've covered to get to the end.

Small Victories

The value of small victories is difficult to overstate. We all want to succeed at something, to feel value, worth, and self-confidence. If you aren't succeeding at something, you'll soon find something else to succeed at. This is where many planning methods fail. You discover your dreams, you write down your goals, and by the middle of the year, you're looking at what feels like a wasted year where you haven't achieved your goals. This is because you haven't had small victories to keep you going. I set this PLAN system up similar to large companies with strategizing, milestones to show progress, and an autopilot that is easily achieved. When a large company does planning it has to have goals that can be executed from the CEO to the janitor. If the goal is increasing the safety rating of the company in the eyes of OSHA the janitor has to be able to execute the company plan. This means planning, milestones, and an autopilot so that safety isn't something the janitor thinks about doing...it's his job and the way he does it.

With enough small victories, and after a month of executing calendar alarms something important will change in you. Your feelings of success will snowball and you'll physically manifest the feelings of success. People will see you differently, see a pep in your step, hear a little more confidence in your voice, and notice you act a little differently. Like someone who's got the big sale, built the perfect table, or had a child win the big game...you'll look proud. If you make your life about small successes this feeling will never leave.

Driving to New Mexico

Outside of my home state of Georgia, New Mexico is my favorite state in the US. While I have driven cross country in the USA many times, I take a different route when I am driving to see family in New Mexico. Cross-country driving is an adventure everyone should experience. I drive from Atlanta to Dallas, Dallas to Roswell NM, in 2-3 days. There's so much to see, and so many areas where your GPS doesn't work, without a map, you can become lost quickly.

From Atlanta to Dallas is the halfway point in this trip, but before Dallas comes Shreveport. At Shreveport you are only a few hours from Dallas, but having driven seven hours from Atlanta, you want to quit driving. There's only one problem with this: when you wake up in the morning and drive from Shreveport to Dallas, that few hours will turn to 5 hours due to traffic. As you make it past Dallas you will run into a variety of traffic problems during the day going to Roswell, NM and by the end of the day you will fall short of Roswell and spend the night in Lubbock. So, if you make it to Dallas, you're making great time and up for an easy ride...but if you stop in Shreveport, tired and thinking 'I'll make it up tomorrow', you've added another day on to your trip.

What do my cross-country driving habits have to do with planning? Planning for 6 months is a reasonable amount of time because at a certain point, at month 5, you will come to your own personal growth Shreveport. You're so close, but you're tired of the alarms, always working on something you put together months ago. You'll ask what did you know back then and why is you from the past it telling you today what to do? But, with Dallas just over the horizon, you'll push forward and pull into Dallas ready to sleep and happy you made the trip.

But, if you plan incorrectly, and make your target Abilene, which is over two hours past Dallas...you'll stop in Shreveport because you won't see the end in sight. It will seem too far away, your eyes too heavy, and the signs for Duck Dynasty everywhere in Shreveport will overwhelm you! You'll pull into the hotel feeling every bump, every swerve of your steering wheel.

This is why we set our waypoints monthly, weekly, and daily...but for only six months so there is an end in sight. At the end of 5 months you can have a 6-month review session, see where you've come from and compare it to your original plan.

Just remember you set this path when you were clear headed, without the distractions of life happening down the road. You spent a few days planning it out, making it make sense, setting up the route so you could enjoy the drive without being lost. Once you're on the road, tired from the bumps and the confined space, you'll think you know better than you did when you were rested.

You won't.

Plan 6 months out, go to the rest stops, hit the gas stations, stay on your waypoints, trust the map you laid out clear-headed and energized. When you do your planning you are smart enough to know your limits, your failure themes, reality checks, what you could and couldn't do. Getting to your future requires a map and waypoints but it also requires a good driver. You're only as good as the route you lay out, and that route is only as good as your ability to drive it without getting tired and running off the road.

Now what...

We're done with planning the work...now you must work the plan!

Let's take a look back for a moment. You took the old map you had, full of information, and transferred it over to a new map. You discovered why you always got lost and how to not end up lost again. You decided where to go and everything you knew about where you wanted to go. You figured out who you could be in 5 years and if where you are going helped you along that path. You figured out if you could go there quickly because of who you know, what you know, how you know it, etc. Then you set it all up on the new map, set out your waypoints for your GPS, and now you're on autopilot. In 6 months from now you'll be a new person, having accomplished some of your goals and on your way to new ones.

In 6 months come back, look at what you've accomplished, and decide what to keep or change. You'll find that you have undone a lot of the past's hold on you and the damage it creates. Keeping on the path you set will stop you from stepping off into the forest where your failure themes and distractions rule. On the path you know what is there, you can see what is ahead, you can prepare for it. Off the path, in the forest, lies danger when it comes to your goals and dreams. We'll have an addendum coming on this part of the process but for now you've got 6 months to focus on.

Focus on the everyday actions, that path, you need to take to achieve your dreams. Trust the process and enjoy your life. Live around your dreams, don't dream around your living. Always hold out a little longer than the draw of the distraction, complete the tasks you've set for yourself, then allow life to distract you. But first, before all else, complete your little tasks so when you come up to the end of the week, month, or year, you've accomplished your goals despite life doing its best to get in your way.

You can do this.

You can undo the damage of the past by understanding it's themes and focusing on the future.

You've accomplished so much unfocused...just think of what you can do while focused.

...now undo the ties of the past and go live your future dreams.

****

The Workbook

Workbook portion begins here.

Page numbers refer to page numbers within the workbook.

If you need to print more pages, go to this link: http://pramek.com/undodownload and you'll find a full copy of the workbook that you can print.

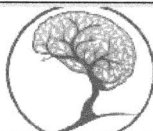

The Workbook

Are you missing a piece?

This workbook was designed to be used with the book Plan. If you are lacking the accompanying 58 pages of content that explains how to use this workbook then go to Pastless.net and find the book and download it. It will make this workbook make a lot more sense if you have the accompanying book. This is an indepth process and we want to make sure you get the most out of it as you work through it.

Welcome to the Future

After writing books on learning that sold by the thousands, even creating interactive books with embedded instructional videos, I decided to poll the readers.

The question was simple...'What could I have done better?

The answer was always: *I wish you would have made a workbook I could follow.*

So, for this book, I decided that a workbook was critical to making this actionable!

The workbook is a guide to help you be the best you...the future you.

Be Honest

If you're gonna change your life, you first have to be honest about where your life is!

As you read the book, use the workbook, and start your path remember your most important ally: honesty.

If you aren't honest your planning will never be successful! So be honest...be candid...be authentic.

You'll be glad you did.

Stay On It

The guiding principle of this system is *plan your work, work your plan.*

I will help you with a guide, ideas, a workbook, an app - but I can't make you do it!

Only you can recognize daily tasks create a life's work.

You have the chance to make a difference in your own life...not chance, not luck, not accidents...you. You make the decisions, you are in charge of your life if you stay on it.

Getting started...

Don't rush. When you free write, take some extra time to sort your thoughts.

Take your time on each page, think through the questions, and don't rush.

If you can't take the time one day, don't rush! Pick it up the next day.

When you start off just remember you're making life decisions here - it's thorough and serious because you should live a thorough life! Experience everything you can, enjoy so you never have to say...'one day', you'll say 'I remember when.' Get started!

PHASE 1: REFLECT

All of us every single year, were a different person . .
I dont think were the same person all our lives
. Steven Spielberg

SUCCESS LIST FREE WRITING

3

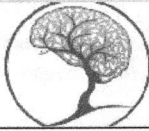

Failure is the key to success ..
each mistake teaches us something
_ Morihei Ueshiba

FAILURE LIST FREE WRITING
Listing your failures is vital to discovering who you might have been...

Failure is an event.
Failure is only an
incomplete success.
Be candid here and
remember you learn
from failure.

4

104

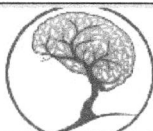

> Success is how high you bounce when you hit bottom.
> _ George S. Patton

QUESTIONS TO PONDER...

How many successes did you previously list as a goal?

_____
_____

How many failures did you previously list as a goal?

_____
_____

Which successes could you have made larger if you had taken more time on them?

_____
_____

What events began successes but your lack of follow through made them failures?

_____
_____

What success events that began as failures, but you turned them around?

_____
_____

Which failures do you truly regret not being successful at?

_____
_____

Which successes have you been working on for a long period of time?

_____
_____

Which failures have you failed when you've previously listed goals?

_____
_____

List any failure events that weeks or months later made you say, 'I'm a failure.'

_____
_____

Which failures did you work at consistently, yet didn't achieve the goal?

_____
_____

Don't worry...these questions should be hard and make you think.
If you don't reflect on the past...you'll repeat it over and over...!

5

105

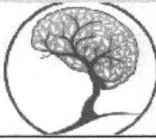

> Success is a lousy teacher. It seduces smart people into thinking they cant lose
> _ Bill Gates

ORGANIZED SUCCESS LIST

_____   _____   _____
_____   _____   _____
_____   _____   _____
_____   _____   _____
_____   _____   _____
_____   _____   _____
_____   _____   _____
_____   _____   _____
_____   _____   _____

Take a moment if you need to, then keep writing...

_____   _____   _____
_____   _____   _____
_____   _____   _____
_____   _____   _____
_____   _____   _____
_____   _____   _____
_____   _____   _____
_____   _____   _____
_____   _____   _____

6

Failure is a much more faithful teacher
than immediate success
_ David Duchemin

FAILURE LIST

_____ _____ _____
_____ _____ _____
_____ _____ _____
_____ _____ _____
_____ _____ _____
_____ _____ _____
_____ _____ _____
_____ _____ _____
_____ _____ _____
_____ _____ _____

Take a moment if you need to, then keep writing...

_____ _____ _____
_____ _____ _____
_____ _____ _____
_____ _____ _____
_____ _____ _____
_____ _____ _____
_____ _____ _____
_____ _____ _____
_____ _____ _____

7

PHASE 2: THEMES

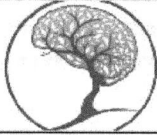

Act without expectation
_ Lao Tzu

SUCCESS THEME FREE WRITING

9

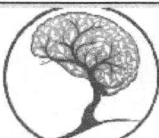

The biggest themes of life are put into the best focus when held up against the very sharp light of mortality
_ Mitch Albom

SUCCESS THEMES

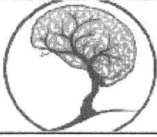

> Sometimes by losing a battle
> you find a new way to win the war.
> .. Donald Trump

FAILURE THEMES FREE WRITING

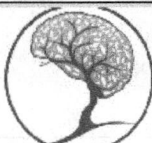

> Failure is not the opposite of success.
> It is part of success...
> _ Unknown

FAILURE THEMES

List the failure themes caused by the factors listed below:

Bad habits: _____

The way you were taught: _____

Peer pressure: _____

Other: _____

What are two failures that you feel were most effected by your failures themes? _____

_____

What two successes were most effected by your failure themes? _____

_____

How often did your failure themes cause successes to be less impactful? _____

_____

List any person you feel contributes to your failure themes and why: _____

_____

PHASE 3: CORRECT

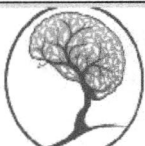

There is only one success ...
to be able to spend your life in your own way.
. Christopher Morley

THEME QUESTIONS

Is there a success theme that relates to your success more often than others?
If so, what is it? Why?

_____
_____
_____

Is there a failure theme that relates to your failures more often than others?
If so, what is it? Why?

_____
_____
_____

Is there a failure that prevented you from gaining more successes, or making your
successes more powerful? If so, what is it? Why?

_____
_____
_____

Is there a failure theme that you feel is more powerful than any of your success themes?
If so, what and why?

_____
_____
_____

Is there a success theme that you feel is so powerful it could help you overcome any of
your failure themes? If so, what is it? Why?

_____
_____
_____

Is there some action you can do on a daily basis to prevent your biggest failure theme
from affecting your life? If so, what is that action? Why would it work?

_____
_____

Is there some action you can do on a daily basis to apply a success theme to your failure
themes that would reduce their affect on your life? If so, what is it? Why would this
theme work best? _____
_____

14

114

Let me tell you the secret that has led me to my goal
My strength lies solely in my tenacity
_ Louis Pasteur

FAILURE THEME CORRECTION

Failure Theme   Action Plan

NOTES

PHASE 4: GOALS

> Each experience I go through _ marriage, my public life, my personal life _ Im learning as I go.
> _ Jason Sudeikis

GOAL FREE WRITING

17

117

> The sooner you accept the fact that you will have both successes and failures, the easier it will be to get your business and personal life headed in the right direction
> . Harvey Mackay

GOAL FREE WRITING

> Greatness is not measured by what a man or woman accomplishes, but by the opposition he or she has overcome to reach his goals
> _ Dorothy Height

GOAL ORGANIZATION

It's time to take your free writing and turn it into an organized list. Organize your goal freewriting in the left column and then refine them further in the right column if need be.

Organized List   Refined List

_____   _____
_____   _____
_____   _____
_____   _____
_____   _____
_____   _____
_____   _____
_____   _____
_____   _____
_____   _____
_____   _____
_____   _____
_____   _____
_____   _____
_____   _____
_____   _____
_____   _____
_____   _____
_____   _____
_____   _____
_____   _____
_____   _____
_____   _____
_____   _____
_____   _____
_____   _____

Life is not a problem to be solved,
but a reality to be experienced
. Soren Kierkegaard

REALITY CHECK - THE NWM TEST

The test of a goal revolves around it's achieveability. Transfer your goals over to this page and then apply the NWM test for the book.

	Need	Want	Means
_____	Need	Want	Means
_____	Need	Want	Means
_____	Need	Want	Means
_____	Need	Want	Means
_____	Need	Want	Means
_____	Need	Want	Means
_____	Need	Want	Means
_____	Need	Want	Means
_____	Need	Want	Means
_____	Need	Want	Means
_____	Need	Want	Means
_____	Need	Want	Means
_____	Need	Want	Means
_____	Need	Want	Means
_____	Need	Want	Means
_____	Need	Want	Means
_____	Need	Want	Means
_____	Need	Want	Means
_____	Need	Want	Means
_____	Need	Want	Means
_____	Need	Want	Means
_____	Need	Want	Means
_____	Need	Want	Means
_____	Need	Want	Means
_____	Need	Want	Means
_____	Need	Want	Means
_____	Need	Want	Means
_____	Need	Want	Means
_____	Need	Want	Means
_____	Need	Want	Means
_____	Need	Want	Means
_____	Need	Want	Means
_____	Need	Want	Means
_____	Need	Want	Means
_____	Need	Want	Means
_____	Need	Want	Means
_____	Need	Want	Means
_____	Need	Want	Means
_____	Need	Want	Means
_____	Need	Want	Means

20

120

> A place for everything . . .
> and everything in its place
> . Benjamin Franklin

GOAL ORGANIZATION - THE 5W'S

The how is often answered by the questions that surround it. Relist your goals that meet two out of three in the NWM test. Look at your goals, refine them, and then answer the 5W's.

	Who	What	When	Where	Why
_____	Who	What	When	Where	Why
_____	Who	What	When	Where	Why
_____	Who	What	When	Where	Why
_____	Who	What	When	Where	Why
_____	Who	What	When	Where	Why
_____	Who	What	When	Where	Why
_____	Who	What	When	Where	Why
_____	Who	What	When	Where	Why
_____	Who	What	When	Where	Why
_____	Who	What	When	Where	Why
_____	Who	What	When	Where	Why
_____	Who	What	When	Where	Why
_____	Who	What	When	Where	Why
_____	Who	What	When	Where	Why
_____	Who	What	When	Where	Why
_____	Who	What	When	Where	Why
_____	Who	What	When	Where	Why
_____	Who	What	When	Where	Why
_____	Who	What	When	Where	Why
_____	Who	What	When	Where	Why
_____	Who	What	When	Where	Why
_____	Who	What	When	Where	Why
_____	Who	What	When	Where	Why
_____	Who	What	When	Where	Why
_____	Who	What	When	Where	Why
_____	Who	What	When	Where	Why
_____	Who	What	When	Where	Why
_____	Who	What	When	Where	Why
_____	Who	What	When	Where	Why
_____	Who	What	When	Where	Why
_____	Who	What	When	Where	Why
_____	Who	What	When	Where	Why
_____	Who	What	When	Where	Why
_____	Who	What	When	Where	Why
_____	Who	What	When	Where	Why
_____	Who	What	When	Where	Why
_____	Who	What	When	Where	Why
_____	Who	What	When	Where	Why
_____	Who	What	When	Where	Why

21

PHASE 5: DIVIDE & CONQUER

5 YEAR PLANNING

Answer these questions about how you've changed in 5 years:

Car you owned 5 years ago: _____   The car you own today: _____

Address you lived 5 years ago: _____   The place you lived today: _____

Job you had 5 years ago: _____   The job you had today: _____

Money in the bank 5 years ago: _____   Money in the bank today: _____

Partner or spouse 5 years ago: _____   Partner or spouse today: _____

How are the following areas of your life different than they were 5 years ago:

Personal Life: _____
_____

Business Life: _____
_____

Finances: _____
_____

Hobbies and Interests: _____
_____

What is one piece of advice your today-self would give your past-self from 5 years ago? _____
_____
_____

What is one piece of advice you, 5 years ago, would tell you today? _____
_____
_____

What kind of person do you see yourself being in 5 years? _____
_____

What do you think your future-self of 5 years from now would tell you today? _____
_____

What is one life change, if you made it today, would give you the best chance at achieving your
5 year goal? _____
_____

The past cannot be changed
The future is yet in your power.
- Mary Pickford

5 YEAR COMPARISON

List out any goals that you feel could lead to achieving the answers above. As you do so, think about how your goals may need further refining in terms of your 5 year goals. If you wish you can begin working backward from your 5 year goal and list these items as goals for the year.

_____
_____
_____
_____
_____
_____
_____
_____
_____
_____
_____
_____
_____
_____
_____
_____
_____

Thought exercise

What goals in your life have you already achieved that are in line with your 5 year goals?
_____
_____
_____

How do you feel these goals will help you achieve your 5 year goals?
_____
_____
_____

How do these goals compare to your goals from 5 years ago?
_____
_____
_____

24

124

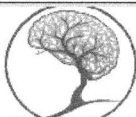

The desire to succeed, the urge to reach your full potential...
these are the keys that will unlock the door to personal
excellence
. Confucius

PERSONAL LIFE GOALS

You might have listed some personal life goals...but perhaps they need a double check! Use these quesitons as a means of seeing if your personal life goals address some commonly held goals other students have wanted to gain.

If I needed to borrow $50 right now, I could call _____ for help.
If my car broke down right now, I could call _____ for help.
If my computer malfunctioned, I could call _____ for help.
If my heart was broken, I could call _____ for help.

Now, contact all of these people and tell them you appreciate them as a friend in your life. With that done, let's look at some personal life food for thought...

When I die, I want people to say _____ about me.
I have always said I would _____ before I die.
I have always said I would travel to _____ before I die.
I have always said I would learn to _____ before I die.
I have always said I would watch _____ before I die.
I have always said I would read _____ before I die.
I have always said I would see the works of _____ before I die.
I have always said I would meet _____ before I die.
I have always said I would own _____ before I die.

If I had $500 I would _____.
If I had $1,000 I would _____.
If I had $5,000 I would _____.
If I had $10,000 I would _____.
If I had $100,000 I would _____.
If I had $1,000,000 I would _____.
If money were no object, I would _____.

I have always wanted to _____ at the ocean.
I have always wanted to _____ in the mountains.
I have always wanted to find out what happened to _____ from my childhod.
I have always wanted to teach _____.
I have always wanted to _____ full time for a living.
I have always wanted to _____ even though it scares me.
I have always wanted to go to _____ if I had a free plane ticket.

So...
How do your personal goals match up to these questions?

25

125

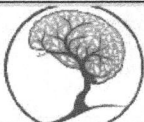

BUSINESS GOALS

Business goals can take up a lot of your time. Whether you own your own business, work two jobs, or you are looking to pick up a new career - having business goals is important. Remember to circle Yes or No when the words are presented!

What goals did you list in other categories that are connected to your business goals? _____
_____
_____
_____

Cirlce which do you dislike more currently

Job	Boss
Career	Company
Position	Department
Hours scheduled	Schedule

How do these answers show you the difference between your job and your career? _____
_____
_____

If you made changes in the areas your dislike, how would this affect you in five years? Would you be more successful? _____
_____

Do you see yourself in your current career 5 years from now (remember, a career is not a job)?
Yes   No

If your career requires training to be more successful, what kind of training? _____
_____ Is this training listed in your goals?   Yes   No

What would you need in terms of time and money to attend such training? _____
_____

What could you do starting today to become more success in your business life? _____
_____

Have you recently looked at a kind of business online that you would like to open or try to do?
Yes   No   If so, what kind and do your goals reflect this kind of business? _____

Do your 5W's affect the answers above? Yes   No If so, how, and how do your goals reflect this information? _____
_____ 26

126

Stay on top of your finances
Dont leave that up to others
_ Leif Garrett

FINANCIAL GOALS

Financial Goals

What goals did you list in other categories that are connected to your financial goals? _____
_____
_____
_____

Are you currently able to pay all of your bills and have money left over each month?   Yes
No   If so, how much do you have left over? _____ Do you have a goal for this money?
_____
_____

Do you feel your finances match your lifestyle?   Yes   No   If not, could you change your
lifestyle to reflect your finances?   Yes   No   Do your goals reflect this, if so, which ?___
_____
_____

Do you have an emergency savings funds?   Yes   No   If so, could you expand the amount
you have saved, or invest it?   Yes   No   If not, what changes could you make to create an
emergency savings fund? _____

How much debt do you currently have in ratio to your income? _____ Do you feel
this is an acceptable amount?   Yes   No   Could you improve this amount, or atleast create
goals to stop it from increasing? _____

Could you become debt-free in the next five years if you really wanted to?   Yes   No
If so, when is the soonest your could do so? _____   If not, how could you change your
goals to address being debt-free in your goals? _____

Have you met with a financial advisor in the past year?   Yes   No   If so, do your listed goals
match their advice?   Yes   No   If not, have you listed this as a goal? _____

Do you know how much money you need to retire?   Yes   No   If so, which of your goals
match your plan for retirement? _____

If not, can you align them to meet this goal? _____
_____

27

127

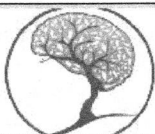

A hobby a day keeps the doldrums away
Phylis McGinley

HOBBIES / INTERESTS

What goals did you list in other categories that are connected to your hobbies/interests goals?
_____
_____
_____
_____

What hobbies do you currently have that could turn into a profitable business if you knew how?
_____
_____

Who do you know that is currently involved in a hobby or topic you are interest in that you could talk to before pursuing the hobby or interest? _____

Is there one particular interest you have that you have wanted to pursue since you were a child? If so, which was it, and why that interst? _____
_____

Are there certain hobbies you engage in that currently take up a large amount of time that you could replace with a new hobby? If so, which? _____
_____
_____

How often do you decide to find a new hobby or interest? Yes   No   Are there certain goals that are so expensive that if you get bored it was have a large cost impact? If so, which and why? _____
_____

When you discover a new hobby do you tend to share it with others, or want to achieve it on your own? Have you listed goals where partners would make the goal more achievable? _____
_____

In looking at your hobbies, are the ones you are more interested in located locally or are they virtual and require travel? If they are virtual or reqiure travel, are you willing to dedicate resources to travel?   Yes   No
Can you become proficienct at this hobby without local representation?   _____
_____
_____

You're doing great...keep it up.
- *Future You*

28

128

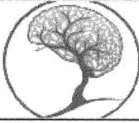

> Awareness requires a rupture with the world we take for granted: then old categories of experience are called into question and revised.
> . Shoshana Zuboff

PERSONAL	BUSINESS

FINANCE	HOBBY

29

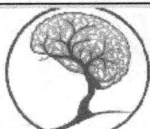

> Setting goals is the first step in turning
> the invisible into the visible
> _ Tony Robbins

TOTAL GOAL ORGANIZATION (TGO)

Transfer the goals listed in your categories here, but now circle the forces that apply.

Personal

N	W	M	Who	What	When	Where	Why	5
N	W	M	Who	What	When	Where	Why	5
N	W	M	Who	What	When	Where	Why	5
N	W	M	Who	What	When	Where	Why	5
N	W	M	Who	What	When	Where	Why	5
N	W	M	Who	What	When	Where	Why	5
N	W	M	Who	What	When	Where	Why	5
N	W	M	Who	What	When	Where	Why	5
N	W	M	Who	What	When	Where	Why	5

Business

N	W	M	Who	What	When	Where	Why	5
N	W	M	Who	What	When	Where	Why	5
N	W	M	Who	What	When	Where	Why	5
N	W	M	Who	What	When	Where	Why	5
N	W	M	Who	What	When	Where	Why	5
N	W	M	Who	What	When	Where	Why	5
N	W	M	Who	What	When	Where	Why	5
N	W	M	Who	What	When	Where	Why	5
N	W	M	Who	What	When	Where	Why	5

Financial

N	W	M	Who	What	When	Where	Why	5
N	W	M	Who	What	When	Where	Why	5
N	W	M	Who	What	When	Where	Why	5
N	W	M	Who	What	When	Where	Why	5
N	W	M	Who	What	When	Where	Why	5
N	W	M	Who	What	When	Where	Why	5
N	W	M	Who	What	When	Where	Why	5
N	W	M	Who	What	When	Where	Why	5
N	W	M	Who	What	When	Where	Why	5

Hobbies

N	W	M	Who	What	When	Where	Why	5
N	W	M	Who	What	When	Where	Why	5
N	W	M	Who	What	When	Where	Why	5
N	W	M	Who	What	When	Where	Why	5
N	W	M	Who	What	When	Where	Why	5
N	W	M	Who	What	When	Where	Why	5
N	W	M	Who	What	When	Where	Why	5
N	W	M	Who	What	When	Where	Why	5
N	W	M	Who	What	When	Where	Why	5

30

PHASE 6: PREPARE

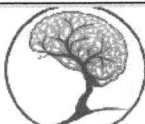

31

The past, the present and the future are really one . . they are today
. Harriet Beecher Stowe

DECLARATIVE STATEMENTS

Declarative statements are vital to success. While comparison language reminds us of the past, declarative language is future-facing. It is a statement about the future, with little regard to the past.

With the previous page in mind, answer these declarative statements:

In 5 years I will be the kind of person who is _____
_____

This year, one goal I will achieve in my personal life is _____
_____

This year, one goal I will achieve in my business life is _____
_____

This year, one goal I will achieve in my financial life is _____
_____

This year, one goal I will learn through my hobbies is _____
_____

I will change _____ about myself so that I can achieve my goals.

When I have difficulties achieveing my goals, I will call _____
to discuss my obstacles and get encouragement.

When I find success difficult, I will use the following success themes to achieve:
_____
_____

My success is not negotiable.

I can achieve my dreams.

32

132

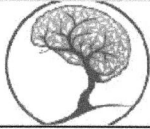

CAPITAL ORGANIZATION

Capital is vital to any business, but you have so much! Now, let's determine what capital you have available to achieve your dreams!

Financial Capital
How much money monthly could you can use toward your goals? _____

Are there goals you could achieve before any others due to less cost? If so, what are they?
_____
_____

Do you have goals that you could share the cost with others? _____
_____

How much could you save monthly toward your goals? _____
_____

List three lifestyle changes you could make that would give you greater savings for your goals.
_____
_____
_____

How could you generate new revenue today, or develop a goal that would create revenue?
_____
_____

Human Capital
Who do you know currently achieving your goals? _____
_____

Who could you speak to or contact that is currently involved in topcs you are interested in?
_____
_____

Who in your life would help with you achieve your goals? _____
_____

Who do you know that you could hire at a low cost due to personal relationships, such as friend's children or students. _____
_____

List people you currently know and what skills they have that could assist you with your goals.

Person	Skill
_____	_____
_____	_____
_____	_____

33

A little thought and a little kindness are often worth
more than a great deal of money
- John Ruskin

Social Media Capital

What domain names do you currently own? _____

What websites do you currently run? _____

What social media presence do you currently have?

Facebook _____	Google + _____
Twitter _____	Instagram _____
Youtube _____	Vimeo _____
Pinterest _____	Reddit _____
LinkedIn _____	Tumblr _____
Snapchat _____	Flickr _____

Blogs you read: _____
_____

Forums you are a member of: _____
_____

How could you increase your social media presence? _____
_____

Time

How many hours a day do you work for your 'day job'? _____

How many hours a days do you have for family and personal enjoyment? _____

How many hours a day could you dedicate to achieving your goals? _____

What projects do you currently have that you could stop and retask your time? _____
_____

List any personal skills you have today that by taking a course you could accomplish large
amounts of work on your goals without hiring someone _____
_____

What courses could you take that would assist you in achieving your goals? _____
_____

What projects do you currently have that you should 'switch gears' and change how you use
capital to achieve your goals? _____
_____

PHASE 7: IMPLEMENT

A goal is not always meant to be reached
It often serves as something to aim at
_ Bruce Lee

HIERARCHY OF ATTAINABILITY

In this section list any goals from TGO with a Need, Want, Means, any 5 W's, and a 5 if available.

1

In this section list any goals from TGO with a Need, Means, any 5 W's, and a 5 if available.

2

In this section list any goals from TGO with a Need, any 5 W's, and a 5 if available.

3

In this section list any goals from TGO with a Want, Means, any 5 W's, and a 5 if available.

4

In this section list any goals from TGO with a Want, any 5 W's, and a 5 if available.

5

In this section list any goals from TGO with a Need or Want, no 5 W's, and a 5 if available.

6

In this section list any goals from TGO with a Need or Want, no 5 W's, and no 5 if available.

7

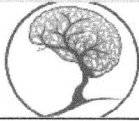

You must see the reaching in your mind
before you actually arrive at your goals
_ Zig Ziglar

THE SUCCESS DETECTIVE TEMPLATE

Name of Goal _____ Expected Completion Date _____

What do you know today about what it takes to accomplish this goal:
_____
_____

How close are you to your goal today? What steps would lead you to accomplish it quickly?
_____

How will you know when you have achieved this goal? What is 'success?'
_____

What do you personally know from research and any essentials you need.
_____

List the following about your goals
    What Websites should you read? _____ What Books do you need? _____
    What Magazines do you need? _____ What Newsletters do you need? _____
    What Instructional materials (videos, Youtube, etc) do you need? _____
    Who do you that
        Has knowledge about the goal: _____ Accomplished the goal: _____
    When do you have time to accomplish this goal? _____
    Where do you need to go for this goal (meetings, locations, city, etc):
        Do you have the means to get there: _____
        Does this goal require a class? If so can you attend it? _____
    What equipment do you need to accomplish this goal? _____

What capital will it take to accomplish this goal?
    Social: _____ Human: _____
    Financial: _____ Time: _____

Knowing everything above, list some steps to achieve this goal:
    1. _____ 9. _____
    2. _____ 10. _____
    3. _____ 11. _____
    4. _____ 12. _____
    5. _____ 13. _____
    6. _____ 14. _____
    7. _____ 15. _____
    8. _____ 16. _____ 37

137

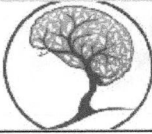

GOAL WAYPOINTS: EXAMPLES

The following two pages are examples from a friend of mine that he allowed me to use which we have referenced in the book. In his goal planning he decided he wanted to train to climb Everest in a few years, as well as develop his savings.

Goal
Start training to climb Everest in 2018

Current situation
I want to do it but don't have any gear and have done some research

List from Template
Climb Everest
Need clothing
Decide what clothing should I buy first (Article I read said shoes)
Need gear
Should I get a backpack?
Should I get walking sticks?
Need to train - how much?
Where can I train locally?
List your 5Ws

Waypoints
Clothing
     Buy shoes to train in
          Research to make sure of shoe brand
          Talk to Erik about boots he used on his trip
Gear
     Buy a backpack (really expensive)
          Check and see if used backpath is an option for now
     Buy walking sticks
          Research brand of walking sticks
Train
     3 times a week, 2 hours a day on steep trail with gear
          Be able to hike 3 miles in 1 hour on steep trail
          Start with Eleanor's plan (from website research)
          Use a oxygen deprivation mask to simulate thin air (idea found on blog)
     Find steep trails
          Look up blogs for hiking in Maine

38

138

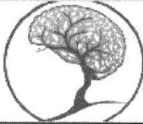

GOAL WAYPOINT EXAMPLE

Here is another example the same client of mine used. He worked through the process and had constant issues with money in a variety of situations. He had established an emergency fund and wanted to do more investments. Unfortunately he constantly ran up against a recurring failure theme: lack of financial organization. As he developed his planning he decided that he needed to have $20,000 in the bank so that he would have money ready when opportunity presented itself.

Goal
Have $20,000 in the bank

Current situation
Currently have $2,000 in the bank outside of emergency fund

List from Template
Savings in the bank - save money every month
How much per month per week?
Do a budget? How much do I need to save?
What can I cut back on? How can I make extra money?
Hold a garage sale?

Waypoints
Save $1,500 a month
    Cut back on going out every night
        Only go out on Friday's
        Have friends over on Saturday, or go to someone's house
            Check people's weekend plans during the week
    Switch to diet that is less expensive but very healthy
        Eat at the office instead of going out
            Premake meals each Sunday
        Cook at home three nights a week
            Make list on Sunday for meals and buy ingredients
        Limit order-in to one night a week
            Set maximum amount for take-out food
    Downsize apartment to save $200 a month in rent
        Lease is up in April
    Do not spend $1,000 bonus at Christmas
        Will bonus be more this year - talk to boss and see
        Discuss with financial planner what to do with bonus
Hold a garage sell
    What is best way to advertise a garage sell?
    Joint garage sale?
        Janet has a garage of stuff - would she do one too?

39

139

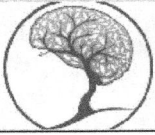

Goals are dreams with dreadlines
_ Diana Sharf Hunt

GOAL WAYPOINT: CHUNKDOWN

January
Buy shoes and walking sticks
Find steep trails in Maine
> Look at online forums, join a few and find a hiking plan to stick with
Research financial goal
> New diet options for cooking at home
Cut back to going out Friday's only
Find new savings every month
> Do monthly budget
> Look at turning hobby into online business
End of the month planning day

February
Buy packback
Begin hiking plan
Do monthly budget
Research downsizing apartment to save $300 a month
Garage Sale Research
> How do people advertise garage sales
> Talk to Janet about garage sale
End of the month planning day

March
Test Eleanor plan
Do monthly budget
Find new plan to achieve goal (3 miles in 1 hour)
Finalize plans to move into new apartment
End of the month planning day

April
Start new program for hiking
Start preparing for move
> Buy boxes, look at renting UHaul
Hold garage sale before the move
End of the month planning day
Have $5,000 in the bank

May
Move into new apartment
Find out if Christmas bonus will be the same as last year ($1000)
End of the month planning day

40

140

OPEN IN CASE OF

LIFE

8 Concepts to Change Your Future

a Pastless EBook

by

Matthew Powell

About The Author

For nearly two decades, Matt Powell's influence has been felt in every facet of the martial art world and fitness world. Training every walk of life, from celebrities to the special forces, soccer mom's to martial art masters, Matt has changed the way tens of thousands of people look at their own capabilities.

Best known as the only westerner to have been selected to represent one of the most technical martial art schools in the world, Matt took that honor and turned it into a science based teaching movement culminating in schools and training groups around the world...all the while being a thought leader in the corporate security world and successful entrepreneur.

Publishing multiple books, hundreds of videos, while working with a variety of organizations and teachers throughout the world, Matt's influence is felt in various industries globally. Matt has been featured in numerous publications, such as UK Guardian, Chicago Tribune, Blackbelt, Martial Arts Illustrated, The Active Times, Combat Action Network, Recoil, Onnit Magazine, and many others.

In recent years Matt has turned his down-to-earth, systematic approach on changing the mind and body toward personal growth. Combining his corporate, entrepreneurial, and teaching experiences into new methods of changing the mind, body, and spirit.

Matt can be contacted at matt@pramek.com

PAY IT FORWARD...

A lot of the books on my bookshelf were given to me, or loaned to me and I never gave them back. I've always made an effort to let people borrow these books, and now, with the books I've written, I have a feeling I have given away more copies than I have sold. One thing I know for sure...

If people need the information in a book like this, the universe will develop a path for them to get it. Nowadays I go through my bookshelf and any book I enjoyed I go on Amazon and I leave a review on the book. I do this because I now know how much went into that book.

So, please...whether you purchased this with your hard-earned money, you found it for free online, or someone gave it to you during a hard time in your life...help other people find out about it by:

Review this on Amazon. Rarely in life do I ask others to do things for me, but please review the book online. The more reviews we have the more people find out about our work.

If you feel you got your money's worth in the content, or you got this for free and it helped you, take a few minutes and please leave us a review.

Join Our Newsletter at http://pramek.com to join our community and get the most up to date information on what we are doing, forums, new products, blog postings, videos, and much more.

Repost on Social Media – post a link to this book on your Facebook, screen shot it on your Instagram, Pinterest, email a link to the book to a friend and ask them to pay it forward. Help us and we will repost if you hashtag it with #pramek and let us know.

www.ingramcontent.com/pod-product-compliance
Lightning Source LLC
Chambersburg PA
CBHW060301050426
42448CB00009B/1707